M
Melancholia

Meaning and Melancholia: Life in the Age of Bewilderment sees Christopher Bollas apply his creative and innovative psychoanalytic thinking to various contemporary social, cultural and political themes.

This book offers an incisive exploration of powerful trends within, and between, nations in the West over the past two hundred years. The author traces shifts in psychological forces and "frames of mind" that have resulted in a crucial "intellectual climate change". He contends that recent decades have seen rapid and significant transformations in how we define our "selves", as a new emphasis on instant connectedness has come to replace reflectiveness and introspection.

Bollas argues that this trend has culminated in the current rise of psychophobia; a fear of the mind and a rejection of depth psychologies that have paved the way for hate-based solutions to world problems, such as the victory of Trump in America and Brexit in the United Kingdom. He maintains that, if we are to counter the threat to democracy posed by these changes and re-find a more balanced concept of the self within society, we must put psychological insight at the heart of a new kind of analysis of culture and society.

This remarkable, thought-provoking book will appeal to anyone interested in politics, social policy and cultural studies, and in the gaining of insight into the ongoing challenges faced by the global community.

Christopher Bollas is a psychoanalyst and former professor of English. His last book was *When the Sun Burst: The Enigma of Schizophrenia.*

Meaning and Melancholia
Life in the Age of Bewilderment

Christopher Bollas

Routledge
Taylor & Francis Group

LONDON AND NEW YORK

First published 2018
by Routledge
2 Park Square, Milton Park, Abingdon, Oxon OX14 4RN

and by Routledge
711 Third Avenue, New York, NY 10017

Routledge is an imprint of the Taylor & Francis Group, an informa business

British Library Cataloguing in Publication Data
A catalogue record for this book is available from the British Library

Library of Congress Cataloging in Publication Data
A catalog record for this title has been requested

ISBN: 978-1-138-49742-9 (hbk)
ISBN: 978-1-138-49753-5 (pbk)
ISBN: 978-1-351-01850-0 (ebk)

Typeset in New Century Schoolbook
by Keystroke, Nevill Lodge, Tettenhall, Wolverhampton

The story I have to tell is the history of the next two centuries . . .

For a long time now our whole civilization has been driving, with a tortured intensity growing from decade to decade, as if towards a catastrophe: restlessly, violently, tempestuously, like a mighty river desiring the end of its journey, without pausing to reflect, indeed fearful of reflection . . . Where we live, soon nobody will be able to exist.

(Friedrich Nietzsche)

Contents

Preface

The disturbing victory of Donald Trump in America, the vote for Brexit in the UK, and the rise of right-wing populism in France and Germany and white nationalism in Poland have confounded pundits of all stripes. Whilst "we" have known of the growth of the right for decades – hidden in plain sight in the USA through libertarian coalitions led by billionaires like the Koch brothers, who openly advocate the dismantling of all aspects of government except for the military – it seems that the new "gilded age" has taken us by surprise. Simple financial facts – that three billionaires in the USA own as much as the bottom half of the country[1] or that the world's eight richest people own half of the lower half of the world's wealth[2] – now strike the popular imagination as startling.

How do we understand this form of "splitting" – between the billionaires and the rest of the world, between those participating in democracy and those seeking to corrupt it, between selves who have a social conscience and those who do not – in a time when we can rightly celebrate remarkable advances in the sciences and technology?

Freud wrote that the opposite of love was not hate, but indifference. But if socially conscious selves of all classes have become indifferent to flagrant violations of economic and human rights – thus empowering a significant portion of the world's population to descend into an underworld of greed, corruption and hate – is this lassitude in fact licensed by a form of hate?

This trend – turning the other way in the face of open violation of social justice – is not entirely new. We see it in the nineteenth century, in the passive acceptance of the poverty of the working classes or of colonized selves around the world. However, by the 1980s it is clear that Western leadership all but abandoned social justice in favour of un-regulated capitalism and right-wing libertarianism. Reagan's "trickle-down" economics could just as well have been named "trick-down" economics, and when Margaret Thatcher ann-ounced "there is no such thing as society",[3] she tapped into a "me first" culture that had abandoned a commitment to social justice.

This work attempts to address aspects of our psychology and the states of mind in which we find ourselves – why we have got to this point, and what we can do about it – through tracing the history of frames of mind in the West over the last two hundred years. Inevitably, this focus on the changing unconscious factors in group psychology will leave out much else in our history, and this book will not attempt to summarize the intellectual history of the West. It is, however, an attempt to identify, trace and discuss the underlying psychological issues that have contributed to this crisis in the West and around the world. The aim is to offer a vocabulary and a set of perspectives that may set the stage for different types of conversation about our predicament.

The book therefore requests a negative capability on the part of the reader, a willing suspension of disbelief perhaps, as I write about cultural phenomena in a way that may often seem removed from thorough and detailed historical consid-erations. Broad intellectual histories tend to elicit a response of "now wait a minute, what about x?", and there are always exceptions to any general statement. I must therefore ask the reader to concentrate on the ideas that are presented, and to forgive what is not included.

I shall refer now and then to how "we" – as members of the Western world – have felt over generations. This may seem to be a royal "we", and of course no such being actually exits. It is intended as a trope to address the Zeitgeist – feelings generated in the population by the issues of life within Western culture. I shall follow the view of the demo-cratic process set out by John Stuart Mill in "On Liberty", as it applies to the world of "reflective persons". This is a person of any gender, social class or ethnic group who reflects upon lived experience and on the enigmas posed by mental life.

Thus, as we think about what has happened to us over the past two centuries, caught up in the manic states of the late nineteenth century and then in a catastrophic loss of belief in our human values following the Great War, we have in mind ordinary men and women of conscience, fallible of course, and destined to wonder about the course of world events and the part played by any self in what Arthur Lovejoy termed the "great chain of being".

Of course, no individual lifetime has spanned the shifting psychic frames of mind over this period. A person born in the mid-twentieth century took no part in the mania of the late nineteenth century. Is it possible, therefore, to claim that "we" have been through these many stages of loss, mourning, fragmentation and bewildered diffidence? It also goes without saying that these experiences through these eras will have been different for women and for men; for people of colour and for whites; for the wealthy and the poor.

So a crucial clarification needs to be made at the outset. Any society will generate a predominant culture and also various countercultures; it will sponsor many cultural states which we may understand as different mentalities. And a cultural mentality may exist for generations, long outliving those who were around during its early formations. We see this, for example, in the arc of the British Empire: the frames of mind generated by British colonialism in the seventeenth, eighteenth and nineteenth centuries remained evident in the mid-twentieth century, even though the era of empire was over.

The psychodynamics of culture – the sequence of frames of mind discussed in this book – address those odd "dreams" of mass psychology, which sweep up a population. For example, it will be argued that following the Great War there was a catastrophic loss of belief in the humanist-rationalist predicates of the previous centuries. Although certain writers identified this shift, it is not maintained that all people felt this way, but a society's dreams – the history of its culture – will register the movement of psychological states. Although these may cease to course through its citizens as individuals, they are retained and elaborated in the unconscious processes that form the dynamic of social dreaming.

The "millennials" were born into a world of significantly abbreviated forms of communication, privileging tweets over letters for example. It is a culture generally uninterested in examination of the internal world, enthralled instead with the technologies of apps and social networking. They are unlikely to have much awareness of what had been lost to Western consciousness in the decades before their birth. But just as the American constitution bears the mentality of the so-called "Founding Fathers", any society will continue to bear the convictions and states of mind of prior generations, embedded in what Jung sagely termed "the collective unconscious". So, forms of loss, states of grief or revenge for the lost can be inherited through acts of unconscious identification. New generations can feel, with a jaded unease, that the promises made by their society, whether explicit or implicit, are not being delivered.

A simple example of this would be the current disenchantment over the credibility of the American Dream. Seemingly a right of American citizenship, it appears somewhat incredible to those who find themselves shackled by student loan debt and unable to find decent employment. Indeed, if the millennials were to construct a "family history", exhuming the remains of their civilization in order to conduct a type of autopsy, they would find buried in the rubble dreams and sketches of a world far different from the smog-choked landscape they inhabit.

But what about people who share radically divergent views of reality? How can we find a "we" here?

Even amongst people whose individual experiences are vastly different, we find that psychic states are shared by members of a society. Although half of America was acutely distressed over Trump's victory, the other half was jubilant. This book argues that the defeated carry the burden of psychic truth, that they register a loss that is in fact held collectively by all people. In this example, therefore, the Trump supporters are understood to be acting as partial selves, cut off from a wider range of feelings. This does not mean, however, that any group of partial selves provides a fixed identity for any portion of a society. We are all in this together; each supporter of Trump or Brexit represents aspects of all selves.

Millions of people now participate actively in "the underworld". They might be libertarians who advocate elimination of government to pave the way for the accumulation of vast wealth and power by the few; National Rifle Association supporters who manufacture and distribute assault rifles, knowing they will be used for mass murder; manufacturers of pesticides that will kill the wildlife upon which we are all dependent; the pharmaceutical industry that "cures" psychological travails by numbing our psychic worth and identity; governments that support the international arms trade that supplies weapons of mass destruction to small nations around the globe. We may vilify those involved in these deeply cynical enterprises, but in one way or another we are all underwriting the underworld.

So our study is also a consideration of a turn towards cynicism that cultivates indifference to human rights and the safety of our planet. As the Institute for Policy Studies announced in 2017, ours is "a moral crisis":[4] a loss of belief in ourselves that has grown across generations and is now a psychic fact of our lives.

Any psychological analysis of human behaviour involves us in making judgements about the psychotic and non-psychotic parts of selves, about the homicidal and the constructive aspects, about our sexist and racist biases and our more inclusive and tolerant ways of thinking. To identify the disturbed parts of ourselves is not to pathologize people, any more than identifying lethal levels of air pollution in Delhi or Beijing is to pathologize the weather.

Indeed, a predicate of this book is that we all share the same elements in common and each of us is liable to change, for better or for worse. And now, more than ever, it is crucial that we be free to identify disturbances in culture in order that we can effect positive change.

Although a manic high permeated late nineteenth-century culture, millions of oppressed selves were in the doldrums of depression. Although some split the self and identified with the joy of their oppressors (a common enough observation especially amongst the workers in the Industrial Revolution), the engine of mania is built on the projection of depression into the oppressed: into the vanquished, into the colonies and into the working class. The fact that oppressor and victim will form curious attachments to one another – as the white working poor of America identified with Fox News and pro-Trump billionaires – can be better understood psychologically than by means of socio-economic analysis.

The gradual destruction of the world, to which this work bears witness, brings all people together in a shared universe of collective experience. In this soup there are no victors or vanquished: both billionaires and homeless will find themselves bewildered and rootless. The oligarchs who accumulate fortunes simply for the power of power itself are simply fast tracking themselves to a nihilistic emptiness for which there will be no rehab centre.

We are in urgent need of ways to understand and reorganize societies so that culture – frames of mind – can be steered towards more generative paths. We are hampered, however, by fifty years of psychophobia: a hatred of looking into the mind for fear of what we shall find. A symptomatic fear of the word "psychoanalysis", even the wish that it be obliterated ("it is dead – and by the way was a scam"), is only the tip of an iceberg. Rejection of insight and talking therapies expresses a fear of having a mind (which comes with a conscience). But the unconscious solution to give ourselves over to non-human "forces" (market, technological, electoral) is profoundly self-destructive.

This book, then, is an attempt at addressing what we may think of as a "political psychology"; a psychology with which to analyse the psychodynamics of culture in the here and now.

Christopher Bollas
Santa Barbara, California
November 2017

Notes

1 See the report by the Institute for Policy Studies in Rupert Neate Wealth. "Bill Gates, Jeff Bezos and Warren Buffett are wealthier than poorest half of US", *Guardian* (online), 8 November 2017. www.theguardian.com/business/2017/nov/08/bill-gates-jeff-bezos-warren-buffett-wealthier-than-poorest-half-of-us.

2 See the report by Oxfam in Larry Elliott. "World's eight richest people have same wealth as poorest 50%", *Guardian* (online), 16 January 2017. www.theguardian.com/global-development/2017/jan/16/worlds-eight-richest-people-have-same-wealth-as-poorest-50.

3 See Charles Moore. "No such thing as society: a good time to ask what Margaret Thatcher really meant", *Telegraph* (online), 27 September 2010. www.telegraph.co.uk/comment/columnists/charlesmoore/8027552/No-Such-Thing-as-Society-a-good-time-to-ask-what-Margaret-Thatcher-really-meant.html.

4 See note 1.

Acknowledgements

I thank the *International Journal of Psychoanalysis* and John Wiley & Sons, Inc. for permission to use passages from my article "Psychoanalysis in the age of bewilderment: on the return of the oppressed" (volume 96, issue 3, June 2015, pp. 535–51). I thank The Provost and Scholars of King's College, Cambridge and The Society of Authors as the E.M. Forster Estate for permission to quote passages from E.M Forster's novel *Howards End*. I thank Rodolpi/Brill publishers and Susana Araujo for permission to reprint here (in somewhat revised form) my essay "The transmissive self and transmissive objects in the age of globalization" in *Fear and Fantasy in a Global World*, ed. Susana Araujo, Marta Pinto and Sandra Bettencourt. Leiden, Rodolpi/Brill, 2015.

Differing chapters in this work have been presented and discussed over the years. I wish to thank the Center for Humanities of the City University of New York for inviting me to be a guest lecturer in 2011, The Hermes Consortium for Literary and Cultural Studies for hosting me for a week at their conference in Lisbon in 2012, the International Psychoanalytical Association for the invitation to be a keynote speaker to their convention in 2015, INSEAD in Singapore for hosting me for a week of seminars in 2016, the University of California at Berkeley and the Townsend Center for inviting me to be the Avenali Lecturer for 2016, and the Freud Museum in London and the Interdisciplinary Humanities Center of the University of California Santa Barbara for the invitations to give lectures on the psychology of democracy in 2017. I would like to thank Susana Araujo, Nancy Yousef, John

Brenkman, Sergio Nick, Kay Young, Susan Derwin and Ivan Ward. A special thanks to those hosts with whom I spent many hours learning important new perspectives; my gratitude to Alan Tansman and Whitney Davis of UC Berkeley and to Roger Lehman and Erik Vanderloo of INSEAD.

This book has gone through many incarnations and I want to thank friends and colleagues who have provided support and critical commentary over the years. Special thanks to Maggie Murray, Arne Jemstedt, Teija Nissinen and Jacqueline Rose.

Thanks to the people of Tolna and Pekin in North Dakota for their contributions to this book. Special thanks to Julie and Leyland of "L&J's" and to Rhoda and Roger Messner and family. I thank the inspiring people at Prairie Public Radio in Fargo and in particular Doug Hamilton host of "Main Street" for his incisive interviewing.

I thank Kate Hawes, Senior Publisher at Routledge (UK), for taking on this book and to Charles Bath, Senior Editorial Assistant at Routledge, for his skilful work in getting it into production sooner rather than later.

Finally, my gratitude to Sarah Nettleton for her comments and editorial assistance.

Prologue

In *Of Plymouth Plantation*[1] Governor Bradford (who arrived on the *Mayflower*) confronted the aftermath of a disturbing court case in which the plaintiff, Thomas Granger, was indicted for serial bestiality. At the trial various animals were brought into the room and he had to identify those with which he had committed acts of a "foul nature" (355) and those that were innocent.

Granger was found guilty and executed in September 1642. "A very sad spectacle it was", writes Bradford, "for first the mare and then the cow and the rest of the lesser cattle were killed before his face, according to the law, Leviticus xx.15; and then he himself was executed" (356). The animals were buried in a large pit, Granger in a grave.

In a chapter entitled 'Wickedness breaks forth', Bradford tries to understand why men of this faith could commit such acts. He considers that "profane people" (356) might have been mixed in with the migrants, and he suggests a few other possible reasons, but he also turns to a psychological analysis of why God-fearing people might break down and commit crimes. He writes:

> Another reason may be, that it may be in this case as it is with waters when their streams are stopped or dammed up. When they get passage they flow with more violence and make more noise and disturbance than when they are suffered to run quietly in their own channels; so wickedness being here more stopped by strict laws.
>
> (352)

He concludes that when people are forbidden to "run in a common road of liberty", evil "searches everywhere and at last breaks out where it gets vent" (352).

Bradford was clearly shaken by this outbreak of aberrant behaviour amongst his fellow Puritans. Evil belonged in Europe; it was meant to have been left behind. How could it have followed them here?

Strikingly, he does not put human failure entirely down to Satan. He could have blamed the Europeans, pointed a finger at the Native American Indians or cited environmental hardships (the voyage, the winter weather). But he did not. Instead he followed the Puritan tradition of looking *into* the self. He searched his soul and emerged with a dawning recognition that there was something endemic to human psychology that would make the idealism of an extreme, faith-driven movement impossible to fulfil.

In other words, he did something to which his "fellow Americans" of the twenty-first century seem averse: he wondered what was wrong with human nature.

Puritan mentality was predicated on an idealized self, aiming to save mankind through a radiant display of exemplary living that would cure the world of its ills. The combination of grandiosity and self-idealization in turn fostered a violent innocence: in order to hold its position as the beacon of hope, the community had to be pure – the exemplary life was the fundamental weapon against the forces of evil. The zealousness of the believers derived from this position, and no doubt many movements begin with a similar spirit of self-anointed grandiosity. It is, however, an impossible burden and it comes with a price: there is nowhere to go but down.

Herman Melville would play with such violent innocence in *Billy Budd*. Billy, the embodiment of a young innocent man, is bullied by the evil shipmate Claggart, who envies his good looks and his gentle nature. In a spontaneous outburst, Billy kills Claggart, and the crew – to their horror – know that the captain has no choice but to sentence him to death. In the seconds before he is hanged, Billy blesses his executioner – "God bless Captain Vere" – thereby afflicting the witnesses with the purity of his grace. But the blessing is a curse: Billy dies and the souls of the crew die with him.

Nathaniel Hawthorne had played with the same violent innocence in *The Scarlet Letter*. Hester Prynne, a saintly woman, had an illegitimate love affair with a local pastor, Arthur Dimmesdale, and bore a child – Pearl – obviously out of wedlock. She was tried for adultery and forced to wear a scarlet letter "A" on her vest. Hester's acceptance of this punishment gradually turns into more than a tale of redemption: her penitence reveals a profound goodness that distinguishes her from her fellow villagers. Hawthorne deftly turns the tale into a moral fable about how the self-righteous who convict a supposed sinner may reveal themselves to be stunning hypocrites.

The Puritans never claimed to be free of sin, and they supported their violent innocence through ritual prostration – casting themselves onto the dirt floor, proclaiming their wickedness and showing their God how they accepted their subordinate position. This tactic was a form of emotional leverage, and it was psychologically successful. For the next two centuries their sanctimonious rectitude spread across the land and found its way into groups with other religious persuasions and eventually into the national unconscious.

Few in the early twenty-first century will disagree that Western civilization[2] is in psychological distress. Brexit and Trump's victory in 2016 both revealed and caused collective mental pain, but writers and pundits have tended to shy away from Bradford's type of introspection, looking to economics, immigration, geopolitical trends or disparity of wealth to explain the anguish of the political phenomena.

If Bradford feared for the souls of his fellow men who were misguided by government, today's world must also fear for its survival. We face an urgent responsibility: we can no longer refuse to encounter, and to learn from, those psychological patterns – both in individuals and in groups – that are powerful contributors to mental pain within society.

In order to study trends in individual and group psychology that are evident in the second decade of the twenty-first century, we shall look back to some of their roots. We shall start with a brief history of the sequence of frames of mind that have been adopted by the West, in particular those aspects of collective human psychology that began in the nineteenth century. In doing so we shall witness the migration of that psychology from Europe to America and then throughout the globe, as powerful psychological forces have entered the world stage in ways that would have been inconceivable only fifty years ago.

As we move through the opera of our eras, we shall of necessity disregard many of the fine points of an age, concentrating instead on the psychological themes at work in human societies. We shall therefore be focusing on a realm that is both connected to events in the real and also strangely divorced from them.

Just as a person may be unaware that he suffers from underlying depression, a group – a village, city, region, nation or global community – can suffer chronic mental distress without knowing it. What we often see, however, is evidence of how such a depression is being treated. The common chemical forms of self-medication – painkillers, alcohol – may be transparently self-destructive, but less physically toxic means of self-help – fitness regimes, natural remedies, pop psychology – are also intended to dull our pain by encouraging us to abandon a self-guided existence in favour of subordination to ideologies or religions, from the fundamentalist to the fashionable.

When a state of mind is the outcome of an unchanging and prolonged situation, it may no longer be experienced as a mood. Instead it can become structuralized in the internal world, settling in as an unconscious axiom. Under certain circumstances, such axioms, which are based on ordinary psychological features that exist within us all, may evolve into patterns or customs of thought, eventually becoming organizing structures that will automatically generate mentalities or forms of behaviour within a society.

This sort of occupying assumption cripples being. We can see this with African Americans during slavery (and since), when a structuralized depression was passed down from one generation to another as an unconscious principle by which selves were meant to live. In a similar way, the personality axiom of sanctimonious rectitude generated by New England Puritanism took up residence, first in the minds of American Protestants and then further afield, in the form of self-righteous violence. It was transmitted through time without individuals being, personally, necessarily given to sanctimony.

The frames of mind within a social group will tend to shift according to both internal factors – the play work of individual personalities – and external forces. So they come and go. However, when they persist over long periods of time then they are no longer simply moods that affect a society; they can become deeply engrained as ways to approach all aspects of life. In other words, psychological axioms come to constitute the culture of a society as a mentality that defines the group. A certain axiom may remain dormant for decades or even centuries as an unconscious way of thinking that influences the society's frame of mind. It may betray nothing of the affective storm that created it, but when the time is right that storm may be resurrected.

We may contrast these underlying frames of mind with more specific group psychologies, such as those occurring in Brexit and in Trump's victory. With both these phenomena, significant portions of both populations reacted with either a manic euphoria in victory or a serious depression in defeat, to an extent unprecedented in previous elections. Under circumstances such as these, a simple electoral reversal or change of political position may be enough to "cure" people of their distress. However, the emergence of highly disparate and conflicted frames of mind within a population may establish what we may think of as a "logic of the present" that will project patterns into the future. That is, a split of this kind between citizens of the same country suggests a future of grave divisions that threaten the capacity of a population to find the sorts of consensus crucial to government.

In order to think about the future we must review the past. If we connect the psychological dots dominating the transitions that took place from the nineteenth to the twenty-first centuries, we see a striking pattern.

The late nineteenth century was an era of breathtaking energy, launched by the industrial and technological revolutions in the West, which released a collective passion[3] that sponsored unprecedented change in the organization

and function of society. There was an explosion across almost
all fields of knowledge that in turn drove an energetic
curiosity about who we are. By the end of World War One,
however, the optimism fostered by the social revolutions of
the nineteenth century was shattered. Writers and artists
of that era recognized themselves as "the lost generation",
cut adrift from humanist ideals and romantic visions of the
heroic self, and from the sense that society was the creative
outcome of millions sharing some profound project.

In 1926, Ernest Hemingway brilliantly portrayed this
loss in *The Sun Also Rises*. Jake Barnes, wounded in the
genitals, cannot now be sexually intimate with his long-time
lover, Brett. Whilst Jake tries to make a joke of his wound,
Brett is at a loss and cannot bear him to touch her – she does
not know what to do with the sexual passion this elicits, and
Jake is without any solution to their predicament. He is the
embodiment of the Western self disabled by the Great War.

But the capacity to sense loss was annihilated by World
War Two and the development and employment of the atomic
bomb. In shock, loss gave way to a strangely deformed type
of mourning, one that saturated the existentialist movement.
Albert Camus stated the only real question remaining:
should we commit suicide or not?

By the late twentieth century, this deformed response
had morphed for millions into an unrecognized and unconscious state of melancholia: unresolved mourning shifted
to despair, disorientation and anger.[4]

The early years of the twenty-first century demanded
an unconscious solution to the disorientation felt by the last
vestiges of the humanist self, and the information technology age offered new styles of thinking, being and relating.
These broke with millennia in which the search for meaning
had constituted a vital part of human existence for many
Europeans, giving way to the impulse to get on with life and
to live it with as little trouble to the mind as possible, as
recreational pursuits displaced cultural interests. We were
emptied when once we had been full of ourselves, a situation
presaged in the previous century. For T.S. Eliot in 1925 we
were "the hollow men" made of straw; for Samuel Beckett in
1953 in *Waiting for Godot* we were singular idiots engaged

in the aesthetics of incoherence; for Eugène Ionesco in 1950 in *The Bald Soprano* we were passengers in trams, failing to recognize that the stranger sitting across from us was our spouse.

Myopic utilitarianism provided us with the sense that our lives were okay as long as we did not ask too many questions. Through a collective sleight of hand, attention was directed towards belief in certain selective human abilities, such as the capacity to think scientifically or the ability to invent new technologies.

With faith in the ordinary self suspended, it was increasingly difficult to believe in being human. The post-Renaissance fascination with who we are, indeed the wonder of life itself, waned in this intellectual climate change; in its place emerged a certain mistrust of humankind. Departments of literature[5] sought new identities and brands, such as "media studies", in order to weather the growing lack of interest in novels, poetry and the history of Western letters. No longer so invested in examining our internal world and its representations, we became focused on the mediums of communication rather than the content of the conveyed.

Too many politicians pocketed victories and dispensed favours but lacked vision. Millions continued to adhere to the great religions, but progressive theological thinking that reflected a belief in the evolution of mankind increasingly gave way to forms of fundamentalism that returned mankind to an ancient and angry God. The turn towards blind faith betrayed a loss of trust in the individual human mind.

The new entrepreneurism seemed intent on an alternative form of growth potential to that of a life-generating meaning. Since the 1980s, neo-liberalism had progressively abandoned the notion that human beings could guide their future, transferring society's collective ambition to "market forces" that came to determine the nature, value and outcome of the world in which we live. Having given up on ourselves as believable mediators of our existence, many of us awaited the new apps that would surely perceive and negotiate reality for us, allowing our brains to wither in the narcosis of self-abandonment.

By 2008, the sheer pace, intensity and mass of capitalist ventures had outstripped the ability of international finance to control the beast it had created; a beast that now runs much of the world according to a psychology remarkably consistent with Freud's view of the id. The theory of the id and the ego is, in part, a formulation of how selves regulate their primitive drives, and we can turn to this theory in order to differentiate between unregulated and regulated capitalism.

The traditional political categories of "conservatives" and "liberals" may now be better understood, perhaps, in terms of whether politicians favour an unregulated world or one that is regulated in the public interest. Examination of the Conservative Party in Great Britain or the Republicans in the USA indicates that meaningful numbers of their adherents favour ego capitalism and regulation of the economic system, whilst there are others who are id capitalists, rationalizing deregulation and the abandonment of society to market forces. The right-wing use of "regulation" as the go-to hate-word is a sad mirror of abandonment of self-control (self-regulation); if the id capitalists prevail, we shall be living in a society that has rejected the human capacity to influence the world. Just as the psychoanalyst works to help a depressed and hopeless person, if we wish to alter this tragic situation we shall need to examine and understand the underlying paralysis that has driven us to give up on ourselves, and the resulting catastrophic sense of loss.

The good Governor Bradford and his fellow Puritans believed their colony would be "a city upon a hill", casting its pure light across the Atlantic. In the context of their times, this vision may have been necessary to carry them through the rigours of the everyday, but over the centuries it became structuralized into the American unconscious, so that in the 2016 election the Trump campaign could call upon it as a national axiom: he would "make America great again". A disturbing number of Americans seemed oblivious to the offensive arrogance of this claim and how it could affect others. It was just a slogan, a phrase that was part of being American, like "the American Dream".

It is very difficult for any society to rethink its psychological axioms, and when the realities of a nation or a civilization fall short of their dreams this can launch a complex set of psychological reactions, including denial, enraged revenge and a deep sense of loss that can last for hundreds of years in the form of an unconscious transgenerational bereavement.

Rome and Athens were once the centres of great civilizations, and the loss of their empires is mitigated by the acknowledged intellectual debt paid to them by the modern Western world. Their empires still exist in the minds of millions of people who venerate their legacy; Athenian and Roman beliefs and accomplishments have been structuralized into Western ways of being and thinking.

The same is not true of the contributions of the Muslim world. In the Middle Ages, Islamic civilizations brought countless inventions and advances to Europe and elsewhere, and in the mind's eye of today's Muslims the realization of deep dreams fulfilled centuries ago remains a powerful internal object. However, their cultural achievements are largely unacknowledged in the West; embedded in the Islamic collective unconscious is a sink hole created by Western negation. This violent indifference involves a complex set of mental events that have evolved over centuries, leaving the Muslim self-suffering from a profound failure of valuation by other cultures.

These losses go far and deep, and if we are to understand the psychosocial crisis of modern times it is imperative to grasp the power of these transgenerational axioms. If a civilization is in mental pain – a topic to be discussed later – then a population may respond in various ways. It may be in denial of what is taking place; it may respond in a paranoid manner and become warlike; it may retreat into autistic enclaves, paralysed by its inability to change the course of events.

Before the apocalypse of the twentieth century, even those who were oppressed could dream of a better future based on the belief that a greater, more liberated world was possible. The future existed as a vital mental object, an internal structure that both generated and received guiding inspirations, evoking inner resources that could actualize a self's venture into the world. Today that dream is waning.

One of the arguments presented here is that, with the loss of belief in humankind, Western societies have abandoned the individual and collective search for meaning. Arguably, that quest itself constitutes the meaning to be found. The matrix of mind that is "the search for meaning" was composed over millennia, becoming a highly condensed mental structure derived from the confluence of many streams in society, including religion, family and culture. The power and invisibility of this river – the *thereness* inherent in its non-appearance – are qualities strikingly similar to those we attribute to God.

Nietzsche's infamous notification of the death of God may, therefore, be an apt comment on the West's loss of faith, not in God but in the rivers of thought that have guided civilization for centuries. Believing in God may have stood for a sense that we could find meaning for our being.

The wars in the first half of the twentieth century, perhaps the final *coup de grâce* for that belief, heralded a failed process of mourning (exemplified perhaps in the limp consolations of existential thought) and a concurrent substitution of a spiritually driven life with a materialist one. The failures of materialism may have, in turn, extenuated the loss and thereby deepened the melancholia, perhaps promoting an unconscious hatred of those objects that have left us in their wake.

In the later part of this work we shall examine the psychological forces that come into play when large groups – especially nations – find themselves trying to evade contact with mental pain. Although one in six Americans is now taking antidepressants or anti-anxiety medications, we tend to see these symptoms as merely individual; we are reluctant to acknowledge the possibility of suffering a collective disturbance. In fact we may be witnessing a social epidemic of mental pain and a catastrophic failure to deal with this crisis in our culture.

It seems that Brexit and Trump's victory have engendered a generalized anxiety, depression and disorientation, not simply in the USA and the UK but in the West. We can

only hope that these shared symptoms will persuade societies to turn to psychological insights to understand how,
through their attempts to avoid pain, they have impoverished
their functioning and, at times, embraced highly dangerous
ways of feeling and thinking. The chain of mental events
unfolding in the early twenty-first century cries out for
intellectual objectification. If we are to modify unconsciously
destructive processes and avoid the catastrophes that go
with blindness, there is an urgent need for a wider understanding of human psychology. Any psychological analysis
may in itself be flawed – as indeed may be the case with this
essay – but sustained attempts to cultivate a political psychology are essential in order to provide cognitive tools to
develop a more insightful cultural analysis.

The development of psychological insight in national
and international relations is not proposed as a substitute
for geopolitical studies, economic analyses or the institutionalized filters that consider and make policy. I shall maintain,
however, that without a political psychology to deal with
our collective mental issues, our intelligence agencies, think
tanks, regional associations and international organizations
(including the UN) will not be up to the task we face today.
Indeed, denying psychological understanding a place at the
table of group discussions of national and international
issues is a form of lobotomy that imperils us all.

When Bush and Blair went hand-in-hand to invade Iraq
and to rid the world of weapons of mass destruction, they
appeared to be completely without insight into the massive
arsenal of weapons retained, not by the hapless Saddam
Hussein, but by themselves. As they exulted over their
attacks, did it not dawn on them that the WMD threatening
the world were their own? Were they just skilful liars, or is
it possible that, in their self-intoxicated bromance, these
leaders had managed to disable the better part of their
minds?

Psychoanalysts term the mental action of ascribing
one's own state of mind to someone else "projective identification", and it is a manoeuvre commonly employed both by
individual selves and by political entities. It involves a form of
evacuation: for example, we jettison our own murderousness

by putting it into a projectee whom we can then feel justified in murdering. This mechanism will not work, however, unless there is some credibility to the projectee. He or she must look the part and Saddam was a good enough bad guy; and although it stretched the bemused imaginations of millions of Europeans, onlookers were helpless to stop B & B productions from casting Saddam in the war film "Shock and Awe".

It is a sad fact that our psychology allows us to take pleasure in killing, and especially in mass slaughter. Many wish this were not so. Over the millennia people have monasticized themselves, evoking a type of psychic neurasthenia in order to hide from human nature, but this anorectic response serves to deny the violent part of ourselves.

Projective identification has the ironic effect of leaving the projector (individual or group) feeling somewhat emptied, alone and isolated, robbed of the very thing that has been projected into the other. Matters have now become complex: the victor behaves as though he has lost. If he has emptied his quiver then, however much he might exult in killing his target, he is now emptied of weapons. The solution? Massive rearmament – even if the other has already been obliterated and it makes little strategic sense.

And this will not be the end of the projective process. The greed to rearm will then be projected into some other projectee – in the early twenty-first century the candidates for that projection from the West were the Iranians, the North Koreans, the Russians and the Chinese. As these target nations will themselves be caught up in similar projective processes, it is easy enough to see how nations (like people) can escalate their armaments and their war-mindedness based on a vicious psychological cycle that goes unexamined.

We shall return later to projective identification and to other common psychological manoeuvres, mental states or actions that attempt to rid nations of their complexity. Accepting and working with complexity can seem tedious and demanding. For example, the American government is based on a system of "checks and balances" aimed to inhibit any fast course of action. Congress can delay or indeed defeat a president, who can, in turn, overturn a Congressional vote either by veto or by executive order. Meanwhile the Supreme Court has the power to rule both legislations and presidential decisions unconstitutional.

In recent decades, due in large part to the success of the John Birch Society of the 1960s and extreme right-wing hatred of any regulation, the federal system of government has frequently been decried for a state of gridlock – according to Trump, it is "a swamp". Presidents and political parties have attacked "Washington", apparently unaware that these assaults on the system amount to an unexamined attack on democracy itself.

It is easy enough to do this: democracy is frustrating. If it is functioning, it will rarely lead to immediate gratifications as all actions will have been mediated through forms of compromise. Since it is likely to encompass widely conflicting views, democratic processes are usually highly complicated, demanding nuanced forms of thinking and communicating. It is not made for human instincts, for sure.

When the Athenians fashioned the system of democracy, they not only created a form of government and a way of life within the polis; they also constructed a theory of mind.[6] As we shall discuss, the democratic frame of mind is predicated on the reality that, for a person or a group, the consideration of any issue will elicit disparate ideas that may include points of extreme opposition. If an individual is divided internally by conflicted states of mind, he or she may visit a psychoanalyst in order that the ideas can be voiced and conflicting points of view represented and considered, first separately and then jointly. Gradually as they become integrated into a less extreme form of opposition, the self can overcome its impasse and continue to function.

The same is true in groups. Clinicians trained in the Tavistock model of group relations take it as axiomatic that the members of a group (usually eight to ten people) will be speaking for a part of every other person in the group, and therefore for the group mind. They are trained to make interpretations guided by this principle. If, for example, one person becomes euphoric and silly, the group leader might say "the group is giddy with thought". When an extreme or provocative comment comes from a group member, the leader's task is to reword it in such a way as to make it palatable; his or her function is therefore to contain toxic ideas and to send them back into the group in a more metabolized form so they can become more thinkable. So, responding to Trump's comments about Mexicans being rapists and murderers, a group leader might say "The group is worried about what people might intend when they migrate to the USA", thus linking the projection into the Mexicans with a fear of something invasive and life-threatening.

The trends discussed here may seem disheartening, but it is imperative to appreciate that all along, in fits and starts, democracy has been developing both as a system of government and as a model for thinking and collaborating with one another. Psychoanalysis can bring to that movement an understanding that we all share the same positives and negatives in our minds, that aspects of even the most odious person or group are to be found within ourselves in one form or another.

To talk to one's presumed enemies is also to engage in a conversation with oneself; to find the good that is resident in all people is perhaps the most difficult task of all. But we owe this to ourselves.

Notes

1 Bradford, William. *Of Plymouth Plantation 1620–1647*. New York, Modern Library, 1981.
2 Some readers may query the very idea of the existence of "Western civilization". What exactly is it? In a moment such as this – and similar objections to follow no doubt during the course of this book – I will note the objectionable even if there is no reply to a negative: it cannot be proved.
3 By "collective passion" I do not mean that *all* Europeans were caught up in this mood. Indeed, many people were oppressed and living in horrifying poverty. However, without having statistical evidence to claim this, I suggest that oppressed people – ground down by the upper classes – will often revere and celebrate their oppressors.
4 As we shall see, not all citizens in the West were caught up in this mourning. Indeed, when we look at the normopathic

solution to the dilemmas posed by mid-century life, there is no apparent contact with grief for the loss of anything.

5 See David Masciotra. "Pulling the plug on English departments", *Daily Beast*, 28 July 2014. www.thedailybeast.com/pulling-the-plug-on-english-departments.

6 Unfortunately, however, they also acted out highly prejudiced parts of the mind. By excluding women and slaves from the democratic process they enacted sexist and racist assumptions that still afflict mental life and social processes today. Ironically, in that respect, they were more representative than they ever knew.

1

The search for meaning

During the Middle Ages, Europe was relatively isolated. Landlocked for the most part – Europeans did not travel much by sea – it was organized into feudal fiefdoms, linked by related languages and by the Christian faith. Peasants and tradesmen lived in hamlets near the manor house, inhabiting two-room dirt-floor houses and surviving on simple food that would be cooking throughout the day in a large pot on the fire in the common living room. The lord of the manor had better living conditions. His children might be sent away around the age of seven to begin their training: the boys to become pages and eventually knights, the girls to be taught how to be wives.

At the centre of the village there would be the church and the inn or hostel. Lives were fated by bad weather, crop failure and plagues. If there was drought, people would go hungry; some would starve and die. If a woman survived childbirth, her baby might not; an infection would usually be fatal and the average length of a life was thirty years. But the church preached that the faithful would go to heaven. The consolations of Christianity cannot be underestimated; indeed, it is hard to imagine how people could have survived over the past two thousand years without their various forms of faith.

Was a meaningful life conceivable then and, if so, how did selves seek to realize it?

The problem is not a simple one. People with diverse religions and positions in society, living in different regions and eras, would no doubt have differed in their views of what was meaningful. But it is the *search* for meaningful experience, however defined, that is the heart of the matter.

A meaningful life lived within the Christian tradition depended on how well the self lived up to Christian values. Jurgen Osterhammel[1] writes that religion in Europe in the nineteenth century was the "most important provider of meaning for everyday life" (873). It orientated people, "serving to crystalize the formation of communities and collective identities" (873). It was also "an organizing principle of social hierarchies" and the centre of "demanding intellectual debates" (873).

In return for their devotion, the faithful believed that their deity was taking care of them, and they would look for signs of such affection. In the seventeenth century, for example, the Puritans would interpret signs from the natural world as evidence of God's love: a good crop, benign weather, an increase in birth rates, the arrival of newcomers. The search for meaning was a daily quest.

Meaning was also sought in the lives and deaths of those of exemplary faith. R.D. Southern,[2] an eminent historian, tells the story of an unnamed traveller who, in 1051, walked from north of Barcelona to Maastricht and then returned to the monastery of Canigou in the tiny county of Cerdana in the Pyrenees. On his journey he visited more than a hundred monasteries and churches, and at each stop he spread word of the death of Count Wilfred at Canigou. "Our messenger was the bearer of the news of his death", writes Southern, "soliciting far and wide prayers for his soul's health" (22). He left no record of his travels but he carried a parchment on his back, and when he stopped to give his news the people he visited would inscribe their tribute to his count.

For the historian, these writings provide a unique glimpse into the way the differing pockets of culture in Europe wrote at the time, from the fanciful and lyrical verses of the south to the more terse and reportorial accounts of the Germanic world. There is something in his journey that is not only deeply moving but also psychologically informative and relevant to this study. The soul of this count, his remembered being, must be inscribed in historical memory and thus preserved for eternity. The traveller believed in the value of his count's life, but also, implicitly, in his own pilgrimage. It gave him meaning.

Across the millennia if people were asked what made for a meaningful life, most would probably have turned to existential meanings: the raising of children, being a useful part of the community, seeking to serve one's deity as best one could, defending one's terrain against invasions, and so forth. In other words, a meaningful life would have been derived from ordinary aims.

Perhaps Baudelaire finds the ur drive behind the search for meaning when he writes "Nothing exists without a purpose. / Therefore my existence has purpose. What purpose? I do not know" ("Rien n'existe sans but. / Donc mon existence a un but. Quel but? Je l'ignore").[3] That is, the mere fact of existence raises the question "why are we here?" and either consciously or unconsciously we cannot help but seek some answer to this question.

From the eighteenth century, the quest for meaning gradually turned away from religious delivery systems, as "man" himself became the object. The search was less to find God than to discover who we were and why we seemed so problematic.

By the nineteenth century that search had become more systematic. As Osterhammel writes, this was the age of "organized memory, and also of increased self-observation" (4). This was exemplified in the formation of a new discipline, "sociology", that itself was part of remarkable social transformation, as Europe and America witnessed the birth of modern libraries, museums, the great exhibitions, and rail and sea transport in a world that had now been properly mapped by cartographers. There was a cultural explosion in the world of arts – in the novel, in classical music, in opera – that cohered and became part of a new public comment and exchange of views. Meaning was now being produced by highly creative societies.

This was the century in which vast ideologies were hatched that aimed to reconfigure the place of the individual within the newly emerging capitalist economies. Marx, of course, takes central place as a figure who provided a systematic formula for a social reorganization that both took the Industrial Revolution into account, as a fait accompli, and offered a way out of its demeaning consequences. But so too, Kant and Hegel in the nineteenth century, Husserl and Heidegger in the early twentieth century, constructed not simply systematic philosophies, but philosophy as a system. Theirs was an all-embracing vision, as bold in ambition as the technological revolution seemed in its march into the future.

Western civilization had always lived according to imperatives,[4] especially those derived from the Christian path of self-sacrifice and devotion through faith, and from the humanism evolving from the Renaissance, in which symbolic portrayals of our inner worlds promised corrections of human foibles. Books on the construction of character appeared thick and fast in the nineteenth century, glowing even in the dark times as self-improvement promised to change collective behaviour. *Self Help,* Samuel Smiles's book on character development, was published in 1859 and sold 20,000 copies in the first few years. At the time of his death in 1904 it had sold a quarter of a million copies.[5]

The West continued to promote humanist ideals, predicated on a belief in the progressive development of humankind. Theologian-philosophers, monarchs and others wove Judeo-Christian axioms into those of reason, science, commerce and invention. And after centuries of reconsidering the Athenian polis and the idea of democracy, slowly but surely belief in democratic government made progress throughout Europe and America. When, finally, women and African Americans achieved a vote and became participant in the democratic process, this overcame parts of human personality (sexist, racist) that had delayed the full potential of democratic governments, thereby realizing the open-mindedness possible within the democratic frame of mind.[6]

It was as if from the mid-eighteenth century to the early twentieth century a confident movement into the future was destined. An aura glowed over the privileged populations of the West, whose accomplishments seemed to be proof of some divine infusion, feeding societies with the euphoria of ideologies and with material accomplishments that could

only be expressions of "manifest destiny". Even those oppressed by social inequality felt the trickle-down hubris of
rampant colonialism and imperialism.

Given that all civilizations have been preoccupied with
dreams and have sought to understand their message, perhaps Freud's *Interpretation of Dreams* provides a clue to our
search for meaning. Each and every one of us, day and night,
receives a rather special delivery from our internal world;
a puzzling and compelling encoded message from our unconscious to our conscious self. The dream is solitary and
unique, yet it is an event (and sometimes a content) shared
with our fellow souls. So we might see psychoanalysis,
then, as the apogee of our quest for meaning, representing
both the object and the search itself. Maybe the "Freudian
moment"[7] was a phylogenetic accomplishment that had taken
thousands of years to be realized. The Freudians were certainly caught up in the thrill of this discovery, sharing the
exhilaration of other founders – Darwin, Compte, Berlioz,
Baudelaire, Renoir, Pasteur – whose search for an elusive
object of desire provided them with an intoxicating sense of
meaning.

Things were on a grand scale in the nineteenth and
early twentieth centuries, and this included the European
mind. Even modest individuals would be caught up in the
new excitements of each decade – some, perhaps, with a
certain horror – but the leaders of the expansive and multi-
plying area of human enterprise would have seen themselves
and their countries in grandiose terms, dipping into the
transient euphoria of nationalism. Cumulative excitement
must have seemed as natural as progress itself.

Is it any surprise that individuals, institutions, cities
and countries all felt connected by the psychedelic glue of
such a state of mind?

By the middle part of the twentieth century, however,
the world seemed to have come unglued. A sickening sense
that the search for meaning had been destroyed was given
centre place by Albert Camus.

I therefore conclude that the meaning of life is the most
urgent of questions. How to answer it?[8]

Notes

1 See Jurgen Osterhammel. *The Transformation of the World: A Global History of the Nineteenth Century.* Princeton, NJ, Princeton University Press, 2014.

2 See R.D. Southern. *The Making of the Middle Ages.* New Haven, CT, Yale University Press, 1953.

3 See "My Heart Laid Bare" ("Mon coeur mis à nu") in *Flowers of Evil and Other Works*, ed. Wallace Fowlie. New York, Dover Books, 1992, pp. 256–57.

4 The imperatives we were meant to live by were part of the stream of consciousness and objectified both what we did not achieve – or who we were not – and the wished-for outcomes embedded in the predicates of belief.

5 See Modris Eksteins. *Rites of Spring: The Great War and the Birth of the Modern Age.* Boston, MA, Houghton Mifflin Company, 1989, p. 128.

6 As will be discussed in Chapter 11 on democracy, however, including women and blacks in the democratic process is no guarantee that sexist and racist views are thereby neutralized. For sexism and racism, like anti-Semitism, are unfortunate expressions of parts of the mind that have always been, and will no doubt remain, resident in one form or another. In this respect, forms of government or the culture of any society will dynamically reflect parts of our mind.

7 See Christopher Bollas. *The Freudian Moment.* London, Karnac, 2007.

8 Albert Camus. *The Myth of Sisyphus.* New York, Vintage, 1991 [1942], p. 4.

2

The Great War and the manic moment

The great European powers of the fifteenth to the eighteenth centuries – Britain, France, Spain and Portugal – would go to war with one another, make peace and live in comparative harmony, then return to war before a further period of peace and co-operation, developing what Bismarck later would term "Realpolitik".

Although the invention of gunpowder had wounded the age of chivalry there was still the idea that a code of honour existed amongst these countries, even as their men were killing one another on the high seas, in faraway countries or in battles at home. Indeed, this code made an appearance during the Great War when, in the run-up to the Christmas of 1914, warring armies along the front lines would hail one another, engage in affectionate banter, and now and then declare unofficial truces, even emerging from their trenches to visit. This culminated in the famous Christmas Day truce when troops on both sides (German, British, French and Russian) came out of their trenches and swapped gifts, treating one another with respect and regard.[1]

It was something of a tradition to love one's adversaries.

It was the political custom for monarchs to marry off their children to powers in other countries in order to secure strategic advantage, and the effects of these national inter-marriages would ramify throughout a kingdom. And all European countries were, of course, held together by the Christian faith. Whether Catholic or Protestant they shared a common scripture, and by the eighteenth century, with the rise in literacy, populations were becoming increasingly aware of the permeation of European values through the fine arts, poetry, drama and the novel.

But there were things on the horizon that would further threaten the chivalric tradition; the war in Crimea, for example.

This should have given Europe a taste of what was to come. It is often cited as the first modern war – it saw the first use of explosive shells, railways and telegraph – and it might be considered as the war that destroyed the faux nobility of combat that had lasted in Europe for a thousand years. France lost 95,000 men; England 21,000, though more from disease than bullets. And although it led Tolstoy to write *War and Peace* – a vast attempt to identify with the souls engaged in that war – it also inspired Tennyson to commemorate one of the most bizarre clashes between divergent military strategists, in the catastrophe of 'The Charge of the Light Brigade'.

So what happened to push these nations into a war that was to exceed even their brimming imaginations, intoxicated by industry, technology and knowledge, to shoot them out of the cannon of the early nineteenth century into the visual blur of the twentieth century?

In a word, Germany.

At the beginning of the nineteenth century, Germany was still divided into hundreds of principalities with no central government. It was overwhelmingly rural and had little industry. It was only because of Prussian hegemony and the skilful leadership of Bismarck that the country was finally formed in the five years leading up to 1871. In *Rites of Spring: The Great War and the Birth of the Modern Age*, Eksteins provides a masterful picture of the rise of Germany. Before 1800 there were no German cities that exceeded 100,000 people, but in a hundred years the population would exceed the growth and the numbers of Great Britain and France. Having been woefully behind in the production of steel, by the end of the century they would be the leading producers in Europe, selling their steel to the British.

This meteoric development, "characterized by overwhelming speed and a corresponding disorientation in the populace" (67), meant that most Germans who had grown up in rural areas were now living in cities. These rapid social changes brought "a disturbing measure of depersonalization that material well-being could not expunge or rectify" (69). The radical move from rural to urban life, from an agricultural to an industrial economy, well illustrates the manic pace of things in the nineteenth century.

Eksteins' most telling point, however, is easily overlooked. He argues that there was a pattern in Germany of privileging the inner world and the life of the human spirit over the world of the senses and material reality. As good Lutherans, their value was measured, not in the production or accumulation of goods, but by whether they lived a life guided by faith. "In the German classical humanist outlook, freedom was ethical not social; *inner Freiheit*, inner freedom, was far more important than liberty and equality" (67). It is not difficult to see how the manic pace of change might demolish the German idealists' sense of what constituted a meaningful life.

Eksteins takes us into the heart of Berlin as we read of the hundreds of thousands of jubilant Germans calling for the declaration of war. Suddenly the whole of German society seemed to be one organic mass moving in the streets – children, businessmen, police, officers, lawyers, all abandoning their homes and offices. We see a nation burst into a manic state, in a scene of Bacchanalian revelry that reached near social orgasmic levels. And although the Social Democratic Party initially opposed the call for war, as its members travelled across the country they were caught up in the feverish nationalism of the crowd: they changed their mind and voted for combat.

Twenty years before the Great War, Gustave Le Bon's[2] *The Psychology of Crowds (Psychologie des Foules)* was published in Paris.[3] The work seems inspired in part by Napoleon's ability to transform an unorganized group into a passionate and mighty army, but also by the curious observation, made by the English general Lord Wolseley, that soldiers at war seemed to be guided by their own group decisions rather than those dictated by generals (23). Reports from the battlefield provided evidence that there were no clear lines of command and that the soldiers acted as an organic unit following their own drum. These reports were revised by those higher up in order to cover up the apparent chaos, and Le Bon cites a writer D'Harcourt, who "relates ...the impossibility of establishing the truth in connection with the most striking, the best-observed events" (23).

Le Bon's work is well ahead of his time; he writes compellingly of how groups develop hallucinations – as when a group of sailors are convinced that they are seeing men in the water calling for their aid, only to discover that they are merely pieces of wood floating in the sea (20).

Crucially, he identifies a change in the European mind. He notes that the experience of crowds has always played a part in "the life of peoples", but he remarks of his century: "this part has never been of such moment as at present" (1). He warns that this shift in significance is ominous, precisely because of the psychological difference between an organized crowd and any other group of people: "the substitution of the unconscious action of crowds for the conscious activity of individuals is one of the principal characteristics of the present age" (1).

It is in his chapter "Impulsiveness, mobility, and irritability of crowds" that Le Bon identifies the potential for a manic mood to emerge from group life; groups are, he reasserts, "guided almost exclusively by unconscious motives" and are "at the mercy of all external exciting causes, and reflects their incessant variations" (17).

Although he is clearly fascinated by the unconscious dimensions of group life, he is also alarmed by his study. Soon after his opening page he goes right to the heart of the matter: "the era of crowds", as he terms his age, is "one of those critical moments in which the thought of mankind is undergoing a process of transformation" (4). What sort of transformation? "the first is the destruction of those religious, political, and social beliefs in which all the elements of our civilization are rooted" (4); "the second is the creation of entirely new conditions of existence and thought as the result of modern scientific and industrial discoveries" (4). In short, technological and industrial changes had destroyed many of the ingredients that up until that time had constituted Western civilization.

Eksteins' account of the mood of the crowds baying for war in the streets of Berlin could have been scripted by Le Bon's pen. He offered a theory, and evidence, of how in a matter of decades the manic actuality of industrial and technological development in Germany destroyed a country's relatively peaceful and stable social structures, and then morphed into a frenzy.

The heightened mood that overtook the German population was much less evident in Great Britain and other European societies. However, a manic state may manifest itself in various ways. It may, as with the German population of 1914, be expressed in the exaggerated affective states that we tend to recognize as mania. But a population as seemingly sober and regulated as the British in the Victorian and Edwardian eras can in fact be moving at a pace that represents self-in-acceleration. Indeed, if we stand back to look at the arc of development in Europe as a whole in the nineteenth century, we see a manic dimension slowly imbricated into idealizing assumptions about self and country.

This dimension may also become enacted, evident, for example, in the intoxicating hubbub of city life. A manic structure can be "stored" in certain objects within the environment, such as a tram, bus or train, so that even when stationary they evoke in the population a sense of power and movement, much like a Formula One racing car might do these days.

As touched on briefly in the Prologue, psychological states (such as the manic frame of mind) can become social axioms, passed on from one generation to another without transmitting the historical origin of the axioms or the original affective states from which they emerged. They become assumptions, part of a society on an unconscious level, evoked through literature and popular culture.

This certainly took place in Germany during the seventeenth, eighteenth and nineteenth centuries. As Eksteins points out, one reason why it lagged behind other European countries was that its population believed in a special relationship with the life of the spirit: Germans were meant to transcend the material world. But however their manic axioms developed, and however they were "held", the various

European countries each developed their own unique sense of grandiosity, of superiority over others, and the sense of power to back this up. Together these combined to form what we think of as the Western frame of mind.

The build-up to the Great War evoked the manic affect imbricated in Western grandiosity but it also brought home, perhaps for the first time, its corresponding depression. Reading historians' accounts of the fighting on the front lines catches the mood swings of the encounter. Eksteins identifies the types of artillery on both sides and describes the effects of shelling on its victims, passing on to his reader the experience of intense engagement followed by eerie lulls; before he asks "Will the cycle begin again?"(140).

This oscillation is a manic-depressive cycle: unimaginable explosions of mood, concretized into bombs, gas attacks and senseless slaughters, are followed by eerie lulls in which the living on both sides find their dead double lying next to them. Let's read Eksteins to capture this mood:

Is the attack on its way? Have the sentries survived? Are the periscopes manned? For when the attack comes, there will be a "race for the parapet," up the dugout steps, should that still be possible, into the trenches, if they are still there, to fix bayonets, to assemble machine guns, to locate grenades, and if time permits, to man mortars, flame throwers, and other sundry weapons of "troglodytes." One *must* reach the parapet before the enemy arrives.

(140–41)

To live one must move at manic pace; to lose the race to survive means death. Between these two forces – the life instincts and the death instincts – are the extremes of any self's life: we are chosen through the grace of God to live, or we are killed, swallowed by oblivion.

For those who survive the high manic-depressive condensations of battle there can be a type of orgasmic relief. Eksteins reports a survivor's description: "'A man who stepped out of the trenches at that moment and lived through has never in all the ensuing years faced such a climax'" (141).

The sexual side of mania will also be evident a few decades later in the fascist texts that promise selves an utterly pure being, cleansed by a war and genocide that rids the world of its impurities. This manic, intoxicating agenda could not have emerged without the engine of the nineteenth century which promoted a grandiose self (and imperial nations) whose exaltation was predicated on violent difference from the other, who of necessity contained the projected impurities. To slaughter the other, then, is to annihilate all connection with the shadow side of any self.

The battles at Ypres, Verdun and the Somme, in which both sides sustained horrific losses, changed the world for ever. Eksteins cites Junger, who wrote that the Somme was the end of chivalry; it had been abandoned to the "'new tempo'" of armed conflict. "'Here the new Europe revealed itself for the first time in combat'" (144).

This new Europe had reached an apotheosis of mania that was only to end with World War Two.

Notes

1 See Modris Eksteins, *Rites of Spring: The Great War and the Birth of the Modern Age*. Boston, MA, Houghton Mifflin, 1989, pp. 109–14.
2 See Gustave Le Bon. *The Crowd: A Study of the Popular Mind*. Maestro Reprints (no date or place of publication).
3 For the best contemporary analysis of mass psychology, please see Jacqueline Rose "Mass psychology" in *The Jacqueline Rose Reader*, ed. Justin Clemens and Ben Naparstek. Durham, NC, Duke University Press, 2011, pp. 86–113.

3

The crash

Faced with the murderousness unleashed by the Great War, Freud writes to Lou-Andreas Salomé in November 1914:[1] "I know for certain that for me and my contemporaries the world will never again be a happy place. It is too hideous ... humanity seems to be really dead"[2] (21). Five months later he is producing the first draft of "Thoughts for the times on war and death"[3]. He begins his essay with a caveat: he is too close to the war to take his personal views as objective.

> Standing too close to the great changes that have
> already taken place or are beginning to, and without
> a glimmering of the future that is being shaped, we
> ourselves are at a loss as to the significance of the
> impressions which press upon us and as to the value
> of the judgements which we form.
>
> (275)

Freud's remarkable essay could be read as a commentary, not only on the war but also on the unforeseen changes brought about by the Industrial Revolution. He does point to the progress made in the nineteenth century, but he is overwhelmed by the war and its implicit destruction of the Enlightenment assumptions he held so dear. He writes that the non-combatant is "a cog in the gigantic machine of war – [who] feels bewildered in his orientation, and inhibited in his powers and activities". Freud seeks consolation by focusing on two themes – disillusionment and death – and he concedes that he is seeking understanding in order to help his reader gain some perspective: "I believe that he will welcome any indication, however slight, which will make it easier for him to find his bearings within himself at least" (275).

The "cog in the gigantic machine" would also do as a metaphor for the tens of thousands of factory workers who constituted much of the working class. If Dickens, facing the impact of the Industrial Revolution, could write "It was the best of times, it was the worst of times" and find something redeeming in humanity, with the advent of the Great War it would be harder to hold onto the positive aspects of social progress.

Scientific advances would prove the one salient exception, leading almost all secularists to embrace this new form of hope.[4] Otherwise, it was only by splitting off from consciousness the mind-boggling forces of human destructiveness (whether passive or active)[5] that selves in the early twentieth century could retain belief in their species. "The prestige of European civilization", writes Osterhammel, "reached its peak outside Europe in the middle of the nineteenth century, before the emphasis on a civilizing mission [its self-idealizing claim] came to be seen as increasingly hypocritical in the decades around 1900 in view of the massive use of force in pursuit of imperialist aims" (828). He concludes: "the First World War then severely damaged the white man's aura" (828).

Eksteins is more in touch with the apocalyptic side of the Great War. Describing how shocked both sides were by the sight of their men emerging from their trenches to near certain death, he writes:

Here the hero became the victim and the victim the hero. The attacker became the representative of a world, the nineteenth-century world, which was demolished by this war.

(146)

Belief could be retained only by splitting off the hideous features of human character realized through the Great War.

As a psychological action this is highly effective, and a review of the nineteenth century reveals that Europe had perfected the art of splitting, both in the presumption of itself as a Christian force for good and in the reality that it was using military force to pursue imperialist aims.

Splitting (of the object or of the self) is an ordinary mental action. It plays a part in what we term "compartmentalization", a process that serves the need to set some things aside in order to focus on a particular issue. Usually what is split off is not sent so far away as to be irretrievable.

However, if the mind finds a disturbing thought or mental fact unbearable, then it may banish the troubling idea and lose contact with it. The result is that by splitting off the unwanted, the mind (individual and social) is both diminished and weakened, especially, unsurprisingly, when it comes to the problem of dealing with what has been split off. It lacks the benefits of a mental inclusivity that allows troubling issues to stick around long enough to be subjected to various forms of unconscious and conscious thinking.

A vicious circle may develop if we split off unwanted facts, especially if they are facts about our self. When we rid the mind of distressing aspects of the self that are real – news from the self that we do not want to hear – we then lose contact with information that we need to encounter. This desertion lowers our self-esteem and eventually our belief in our species; it is a self-abandonment that leaves us unable to deal with the disturbing aspects of ourselves and our societies. Not only do we lose our idealized view of our self, we have compounded this loss by ridding our self of the part of the mind that could tolerate our imperfections so that we could think about them.

At the same time, however, splitting and projective identification also *lighten* the mind, creating a euphoria by allowing us to float away from the more sober sides of reality. They can give rise to a heady optimism that is predicated on an absence of self-examination and on a forward momentum derived from getting the loads off the mind.

The optimism to be found amongst some sectors of Western society throughout the twentieth century and into the twenty-first century could be accomplished only by splitting off many issues that should have deterred rosy pictures of the future, and projecting the unwanted parts of self and society into "the other". And a ready-to-hand other was to be found in the southern hemisphere. Osterhammel writes: "At one end, coexisting with the humanitarianism of a morally solicitous Europe, was a calm and arrogant acceptance that 'primitive peoples' were doomed to extinction" (834). So when Europe colonized Africa in the second half of the nineteenth century it found its perfect "other": "savages" would contain the projective identifications of European minds. They were meant to be primitive and violent so that the West could be sophisticated and pure. Osterhammel: "From the point of view of nineteenth-century civilized cities, barbarism was lurking everywhere in the most diverse guises" (835).

In the last thirty-five years of the nineteenth century, 80 per cent of Africa was invaded and colonized by the European powers, many getting a slice of what King Leopold of Belgium called "this magnificent African cake" (viii).[6] If Goethe's *Faust* (1808) can be read as an uncanny manifesto of the material greed and callousness about to unleash itself on humanity in the name of industry and progress, then Conrad's *Heart of Darkness* (1899) seems to offer an end of century accounting for the profound oppression unleashed by armed greed. Colonialism was many things, but perhaps above all it was the march of absolute ignorance, invading rather than understanding the human universe. Kurtz's dying words – "'The horror! The horror!'"[7] – are both an epitaph for the nineteenth century and an uncanny foretelling of the era to follow.

How many Europeans allowed themselves to recognize the murderousness of colonialism? How many Americans who celebrated "manifest destiny" retained any connection with the slaughter of innocent people who were in the path of this seductive idea? By the 1880s the overwhelming power of Europe over the rest of the world sponsored a manic state of mind; fuelled by self-idealization, they licensed themselves to ravage the world. Manic licensing is a crucial step in any society's move from a grandiose state of mind to actions aimed to conquer or murder lesser beings. The world is divided into Gods and heathens.

There is no doubting the unparalleled progress made in the West due to capitalist enterprises, the sciences and other aspects of culture, and there is no fault in being proud of achievement. The problem arises when such accomplishments bring a sense of entitlement that authorizes the slaughter of millions of people.

Those brave enough to face the moral catastrophes of colonialism encountered a terrifying and disabling object of thought, and Conrad, while writing *Under Western Eyes* (1911), lost his mind through over-identifying with his fictional characters. For those prepared to undo the split and see the whole picture, to imagine Western civilization could be to jeopardize one's sanity. These were times made frantic by the collision between movements of secular belief (romanticism, naturalism, impressionism) and the mentally dispersing effect of mechanization and urbanization. In 1888, in his preface to *Miss Julie*[8] (subtitled "A Naturalistic Tragedy"), August Strindberg hailed the arrival of the "age of transition". "Modern characters", he argues, are "more urgently hysterical" than those of the preceding age, and as a result those who populate his plays are "more split and vacillating" (59). He concludes:

> My souls (characters) are conglomerates of past and
> present stages of culture, bits out of books and
> newspapers, scraps of humanity, torn shreds of once fine
> clothing, now turned to rags, exactly as the human soul
> is patched together . . .
>
> (60)

Strindberg is identifying another aspect of splitting: it devastates the integrative capacity of any self, leaving souls "vacillating" from one position to another. (Later, I shall contrast this with the democratic mind, which aims to hold and tolerate all its differing elements so that nothing is eliminated. Invested with attending to all parts, the democratic process makes use of vacillation as a mental activity devoted to moving back and forth between all parts of a mind.)

Strindberg identified the fragmentation that was beginning to split open centuries of European hegemony built around interconnecting axioms.

And then came Nietzsche.

Ignored for the most part by his fellow Germans, Nietzsche would be discovered by the Danish critic George Brande (also something of an impresario), inspiring a correspondence between Nietzsche and Strindberg that shoved Nietzsche into the limelight across Europe. As Bradbury and McFarlane[9] discuss, no writer had ever had such a flashing success across so many countries in such a brief span of time; this was in itself an ironic prefiguration of an era that was about to overwhelm its thinkers with its own ineluctable speed. The cadence of Nietzsche's passions moved like the inexorable force he so derided in Europe, as if his mood had no choice.

In 1888 Strindberg had written of "tatters of clothing", and sometime between 1937 and 1939, in "The Circus Animals' Desertion", Yeats would describe selves living in the "rag and bone shop of the heart".[10]

Between 1888 and 1925 European intellectuals who had inherited a belief in social progress, first in the Nordic countries, then in Germany, then in France and England, witnessed the mental, social and cultural perils of industrialism. Then they saw how the Great War shattered the efforts of movements such as impressionism, imagism and futurism to cohere a collective mind, so that it might transform the hideous through that redemption implicit in retrospective understanding.

In his *Autobiography*, Yeats observes the "growing murderousness of the world".[11] Pondering the Great War in 1919, in "The Second Coming", perhaps the most visionary poem ever composed, he writes:

> The blood-dimmed tide is loosed and everywhere
> The ceremony of innocence is drowned.[12]

Murderousness is as old as our species, but this outburst was not as simple as it sounds. The murderous frame of mind, although latent in all of us, must be triggered by some psychic or existential factor in order to become a reality. In the situation we are studying, murderous actions are directed by a manic frame of mind in individuals and nations (the mental state that exults a cause before going to war) towards an enemy who holds the split off, unwanted parts of themselves.

But if they have been successfully projected, why then murder? Because the other will always threaten to return the projected to the sender; so it is only by obliterating the other that these rejected parts can finally be annihilated. It is in this act of annihilation – very different from projection – that selves begin to feel a remarkable, cleansing, transcendental power.

However, when the murderous frame of mind licenses killing in order to rid the self of depressive elements, all selves know unconsciously that this form of transcendence can only be temporary. This knowledge brings an increased hatred towards the depressed parts of the self – and towards depression as a state of mind – that further fuels the murderousness as a defence.

Even if the manic society appears to be in an exultant and self-idealizing frame of mind, the irony is that the depression of which it seeks to rid itself is caused to a large extent by a catastrophic loss of belief in its own goodness. A vicious circle is then established in which domination of others must continue in order to ward off the return of the depressed and the harrowing news of that society's violation of its vision of itself as humane.

Yeats's line "The ceremony of innocence is drowned" could be uttered only by someone who is standing outside the manic-depressive process and seeing it unfolding before his eyes. And in all eras there are untold numbers of people who watch, paralysed in horror, as their fellow citizens are caught up in a psychological process to which they are blind. It is the dawn of an age of bewilderment, put well by Ortega y Gassett:

Our own period is constitutionally one of desperation.
What I say is that it is a period of disorientation, nothing
more.[13]

Notes

1 Sigmund Freud and Lou-Andreas Salomé. *Letters*, ed. Ernst
Pfeiffer. New York, W.W. Norton, 1985.

2 It is fascinating and prescient that Anna Freud and Heinz
Hartmann, who were founding ego psychology on the cusp of
World War Two, incorporate war and its impact on the self
through metaphor in their theory of the ego. Japan had
invaded Manchuria in 1931 and was on the verge of invading
China; the atmosphere of war was already present when these
authors were writing their seminal texts. Anna Freud: "When
the relation between two neighboring powers – ego and id – are
peaceful" then all is well and "in favourable cases the ego does
not object to the intruder" (6) but "peaceful relations between
the neighbouring powers are at an end" at times and instinctual
impulses may launch "a surprise attack. The ego on its side
becomes suspicious; it proceeds to counterattack and to invade
the territory of the id" (7). Hartmann: "to use an analogy, the
description of a country, a nation, a state, includes, besides
its involvements in wars with neighboring nations or states, its
boundaries and the peacetime traffic across the borders" (11)
and writing of "the borderland of the ego" "the effectiveness
of the armies defending the borders also depends on the support they get or do not get from the rear" (15). It is telling and
moving that in some respects their ego psychology is itself
an effort of the ego to adapt to and to survive the horrors
of their era. Anna Freud's and Hartmann's works were published within one year of one another. See Anna Freud. *The Ego
and the Mechanisms of Defence*. London, Hogarth, 1968 [1936];
and Heinz Hartmann. *Ego Psychology and the Problem of
Adaptation*. New York, International Universities Press, 1958
[1938]. The finest psychoanalytical study of war is Franco
Fornari. *The Psychoanalysis of War*. Bloomington, Indiana
University Press, 1975 [1966]. For a brilliant essay on the
influence of the events of World War Two on Freud's theories,
see "Freud's study of Moses as a daydream: a biographical
essay" in Ilse Grubrich-Simitis, *Early Freud and Late Freud:
Reading Anew Studies on Hysteria and Moses and Monotheism*.
London, Routledge, 1997, pp. 53–89.

3 Sigmund Freud, "Thoughts for the times on war and death" in *The Standard Edition of the Complete Works of Sigmund Freud*, volume XIV, 273–300. London, Hogarth Press, 1955 [1915].

4 In (2000) *The Modern Mind: An Intellectual History of the 20th century* (New York, Perennial, 2002), perhaps the best volume on Western thought since the beginning of the twenty-first century, Peter Watson embraces Western science as the single most redeeming accomplishment of the twentieth century. One can of course also include remarkable evolutions in art, music, fiction and so forth. The point is not that the world stopped progressing, it is that *on balance* the weight of human greed, destructiveness and indifference marginalizes human creativity.

5 Active human destructiveness, such as genocide, is not difficult to identify. What is more difficult, however, is passive destruction. This is when selves, groups or nations remain inactive when intervention would arrest a destructive process.

6 Cited in Hannu Salmi. *Nineteenth Century Europe*. Cambridge, Polity, 2008.

7 Joseph Conrad. *Heart of Darkness* in *Heart of Darkness and Other Tales*. Oxford: Oxford University Press, 2008, p. 178.

8 The selections from the preface are from August Strindberg, *Miss Julie and Other Plays*. Oxford, Oxford University Press, 2008.

9 See Malcolm Bradbury and James McFarlane. *Modernism*. London, Penguin, 1976, pp. 42–43.

10 See *The Collected Poems of W. B. Yeats*, revised second edition, ed. Richard J. Finneran. New York, Scribner, p. 348.

11 See David A. Ross. *Critical Companion to W.B. Yeats: A Literary Reference to His Life and Work*. New York, Infobase, 2009, p. 220 (available online).

12 See Yeats, *Collected Poems*, p. 187.

13 Jose Ortega y Gasset. *Man and Crisis*. New York, W.W. Norton, 1958, p. 140.

4

Human character changes

"On or about December 1910", wrote Virginia Woolf, "human character changed":

> I am not saying that one went out, as one might into a garden, and there saw that a rose had flowered, or that a hen had laid an egg. The change was not sudden and definite like that. But a change there was, nevertheless; and since once must be arbitrary, let us date it about the year 1910.[1]

An interesting year to pick out of the hat; it was in 1910 that E.M. Forster, her least favourite author, published *Howards End*.[2] This has been viewed by many a literary critic as a seminal moment in the history of the novel and of Western consciousness, and Forster's use of the word 'End' is telling.

The work centres on the relations between the Wilcoxes and the Schlegels. The Schlegel family embodies the imagined values of the English gentry that had somehow survived the mercantile and Industrial Revolution. They maintained a sensibility that could claim derivation from the culture of gentlemen and gentlewomen that had ruled in rural England for centuries. The Wilcoxes, on the other hand, are the *nouveau riche*, not interested in a cultured life, and unconcerned with previous generations. They are ignorant of the landed gentry's belief that privilege has invested them as guardians of the future, obliged to pursue a literate interest in the sensibility of the times in order to sustain valued ideals.

Maggie Schlegel marries Henry Wilcox, a businessman who, interested in material wealth alone, exemplifies a radical new present. As Henry chortles, "I am not a fellow who bothers about my own inside" (119), Forster writes: "It was hard-going in the roads of Mr. Wilcox's soul as he simply did not notice things, and there was no more to be said" (119). Henry's thoughtful and rather long-suffering wife breaks out of her dutiful role in a famous "sermon" that has no equivalent in the English novel: "Only connect! That was the whole of her sermon. Only connect the prose and the passion, and both will be exalted, and human love will be seen at its height. Live in fragments no longer" (119).[3] Although the phrase "only connect" is familiar to all students of English literature, Forster's intention is not always grasped. He does not mean that people should connect with one another – this is not an early step towards modern relationalism – but that we need to connect our speech with our feelings. The loss that Maggie Schlegel discloses is her grief over a failure to imbue language with passion.

That she says this to a husband who is completely un-interested in connecting passion with speech is Forster's way of confronting the new age, implicitly contrasting it with the previous three centuries, when wording the self's experiences and speaking them to the other were crucial to the development of human sensibility. "Live in fragments no longer" alludes to a psychological catastrophe in selves who no longer feel internally integrated. Their inner life – as opposed to what they may say to others –is fragmented because a psychic division has occurred between feeling and speech. It is a rift felt most acutely in our inner narratives as we speak lived experience to our self.

Henry Wilcox turns away from a reflective life and pursues his entrepreneurial career, as did millions of Europeans and Americans who buried themselves in their ventures, oblivious to the exploitation of the working-class citizens and colonized people elsewhere in the world. It was simply the natural order of things.

The self fragmented in the first place because the values that had been the glue of European civilization for centuries – the Christian matrix, the reciprocal fidelities of peasant and aristocracy, the belief in the humane sides of the human being – were broken in pieces in the nineteenth century. However, those beliefs would continue, in some respects and in differing domains, sustaining long-cherished values that gave life meaning, even as the Industrial Revolution, id capitalism and military might unleashed the forces of greed.

Some eleven years after Woolf's statement about human character, T.S. Eliot,[4] in his essay "The Metaphysical Poets", addressed the same issue as Forster. But Eliot placed the disconnection between passion and prose (or rather poetry) in the seventeenth century, when he argued that there was, rather out of the blue, a "dissociation of sensibility" (64). He maintained that John Donne was the last poet for whom feelings were simultaneous with language. To speak was to express emotion – they were inseparable – but after Donne there was a rift that was never healed. Eliot's critique constitutes a type of mourning that derived, not from the immediate, but from reading works from the past; he is feeling a loss from some three centuries before his own existence.

The *sense* of loss is endemic to being human. However much we gain in life, we are always on the losing end. Things never seem to be what they once were and that is probably because they aren't. However, the collective alarm of writers across Europe and America over the Great War, and what it meant, was unprecedented.

When Virginia Woolf looks back, in 1924, on how the world changed for her in 1910, it is intriguing that she does not link the loss to the frantic mania of late nineteenth- and early twentieth-century Europe, or to the Great War, the most savage war in the history of mankind. But unlike Eliot, she does at least connect it to her own era. It seems that we all tend to resist linking a sense of loss to profound present catastrophes – for the Americans of the late twentieth century it would be the Vietnam War – because we are unconsciously motivated to negatively hallucinate (not to see) the most distressing facts of life. Woolf felt that character had changed, and perhaps it had, but our personalities will always be altered by powerfully disturbing events in the real.

The loss that she names is the foundation of what Camus will term "the absurd". In *The Myth of Sisyphus*[5] he writes:

> A world that can be explained even with bad reasons is a familiar world. But, on the other hand, in a universe suddenly divested of illusions and lights, man feels an alien, a stranger. This divorce between man and his life, the actor and his setting, is properly the feeling of absurdity.
>
> (6)

Camus belonged to the generation that followed Woolf. Although it experienced the aftermath of the Great War, it was destined, tragically, to repeat the same march to manic war-making that had marred her era. Camus completed *The Stranger* in 1940, two years after Sartre published *Nausea*. According to Robert Zaretsky,[6] Camus first used the term "the absurd" in a journal entry in May of 1936. By 1938 he was referring to his theory of the absurd and plotting an essay on the topic.

The Stranger and *Nausea* have to be viewed as literary derivatives of two World Wars that crippled the soul of the Western self. In place of the hero, we now have not so much an anti-hero as a negated human being; an absence of self and thought where once existed presence, insight and soul searching. Zaretsky reminds us that the prosecuting attorney, looking into the soul of Meursault, says that "'he had found nothing human'" (46).

The scale of the slaughter of these wars is unimaginable, and this raises a question: how can one think this? More than many other writers, Camus and Sartre managed to identify the internal cost to being human. How does one find meaning in a world that has disappeared? Zaretsky comments on *The Myth of Sisyphus*:

> Though Camus makes few if any explicitly historical or political references, his essay nevertheless reverberates to the cataclysm unleashed on Europe. As a result, an essay Camus first began as his own intellectual and

emotional itinerary soon deepened into a quest for meaning in a world whose values and expectations had utterly imploded.[7]

Camus' theory of the absurd states that we must begin any thought about our existence from the premise that life is inherently meaningless. It is predicated on the loss, in the Western world, of that value to be gained in the search for meaning. Indeed, in 1955, in his preface to the American edition of *The Myth of Sisyphus*, he writes: "The fundamental subject of 'The Myth of Sisyphus' is this: it is legitimate and necessary to wonder whether life has a meaning; therefore, it is legitimate to meet the problem of suicide face to face" (v).

The Stranger[8] famously begins: "Maman died today. Or yesterday, maybe, I don't know." Camus detaches the character from emotional response and, importantly, he links this remove to a loss of the sense of time. For Meursault, the events of life are now dead to him and he can register only sights, sounds and sensations. What matters is what his boss will think of him leaving work, the bus journey from Algiers to the funeral, and the suffocating heat, brilliantly captured by Camus in his description of the perspiration dripping from the bodies of those who walk with the casket down the long dirt road.

The caretaker is stunned that Meursault does not wish to view his mother's casket; his lover, Marie, asks him if he loves her and he replies, "I told her it didn't mean anything but that I didn't think so. She looked sad" (35). And when a friend is bereft over the loss of his dog, Meursault recalls, "I told old Salamano that he could get another dog, but he was right to point out to me that he was used to this one" (44).

The most animated moments in the novel come in a beautiful portrayal by Camus of his character watching the day's events passing by him on the main street of his neighbourhood. It was "a beautiful afternoon"; "first, it was families out for a walk; two little boys in sailor suits, with trousers below the knees, looking a little cramped in their stiff clothes; a little girl with a pink bow and black patent-leather shoes"; a father with a straw hat walking by; then a group of boys, then after them, "the street slowly emptied out" (22). It is the street that is animated, that has the personality, not the people. Meursault continues to observe all that pass by – shopkeepers, cats, a tobacconist, streetcars, a waiter, passing clouds; the "sky grew dark" (22) and later "the sky changed again" – like the street, the sky carries its own actions. These impersonal dimensions are now the life to be found.

Camus continues his description but increases the pace of the observed in a kaleidoscopic way: at five o'clock street-cars show up; fans from a football game pass by; then the players come in another tram; the sky has a reddish hue; new groups appear – walkers "straggling back", children crying, moviegoers passing by, local girls walking arm in arm.

By upping the pace (the temporal) and over-occupying the street with activity (the spatial), Camus condenses space and time in a dizzying way, recalling Baudelaire's famous musings on the excitement of city life. This is a famous trope in French literature, but here Camus adds a new dimension: he splits the viewer's self in two: an alive observer, a dead self. The prose is animated but Meursault is not; just as he is removed from the people he sees, he is a "stranger" to the very prose that describes him. The street and the sky form the background to a sensational movement of objects pass-ing before the reader with an intensity that creates for us a simulacrum of Meursault's perspiring state, as he treads behind his mother's casket on the dusty road outside her village.

It is all too much.

If mother is dead and her death day unrememberable, if a girlfriend's love is meaningless, or a man's affection for his dog easily replaceable, then perhaps life can be found in the movement of strangers in the street. We observe the panoply of the living, but next to us, in the trenches of this reading experience, is the corpse of Meursault, a person who was once alive (we assume) but who is now psychically dead.

The Stranger followed *The Myth of Sisyphus* by two years, and to the question posed in the earlier work – why not commit suicide? – we now have to face a new dilemma: what do you do if your being has died? Like Sartre later, Camus will take a further step towards answering these questions: the solution is to live with the dilemma of being, whatever it throws your way, but here he is conveying the effect of the death of meaning upon the self.

So, who is left to mourn this loss?

The world is still there. The buzz of street life can be heard. But we are no longer inspired – as were Baudelaire or Walter Benjamin or the *flâneurs* of the nineteenth and twentieth centuries – with the city as an animated representation of human creativity. Something had killed us off. What was it?

It seems that the Great War forced us to lose our memory of that vital internal chain of mental events that allows us to gather together the self's present experiences from within the textures of the thousands of moments past. Woolf's assertion that human character had changed was echoed thirty years later by Camus' view that it was now dead. A decade after this, psychiatry would propose a new formation: a self divided down the middle, one part that idealized the world and another that hated it.

Notes

1   Virginia Woolf. "Character in fiction" in *The Essays of Virginia Woolf: Volume Three, 1919–1924*, ed. Andrew McNeillie. San Diego, CA, Harcourt Brace Jovanovich, 1988 [1924], pp. 421–22.

2   See E.M. Forster. *Howards End*. San Bernardino, CA, Cassia Press, 2009.

3   I am grateful to The Provost and Scholars of King's College, Cambridge and The Society of Authors as the E.M. Forster Estate for permission to quote from E.M. Forster's *Howards End*.

4   See T.S. Eliot. "The metaphysical poets" in *Selected Prose of T.S. Eliot*, ed. Frank Kermode. New York, Harcourt Brace Jovanovich, 1975.

5   See Albert Camus. *The Myth of Sisyphus*. New York, Vintage, 1991 [1942].

6   See Robert Zaretsky. *A Life Worth Living: Albert Camus and the Quest for Meaning*. Cambridge, MA, Harvard University Press, 2016.

7   Ibid., pp. 26–27.

8   See Albert Camus. *The Stranger*. New York, Vintage, 1989 [1942].

5

Fractured selves

In 1953, Robert Knight, Director of the Menninger Clinic in Topeka, Kansas, wrote an article on a new personality.[1] He called these patients "borderline" and by the mid-1960s this had become a most compelling diagnostic term, first in the United States and then in Europe and around the world. Then, in 1975 Otto Kernberg (himself on the staff of Menninger in the 1960s and early 1970s) produced what was arguably the most important work in psychiatry and psychoanalysis of that era: *Borderline Conditions and Pathological Narcissism*.[2] No text has had a greater influence on clinical practice in modern times.

In fact, however, if we attempt to define exactly what "a borderline" is, we find it is not so easy, but fortunately the brief here is not to discuss its limitations as a theory of a personality type. For an entire world of mental health clinicians to sit up and take notice of such a term was remarkable and telling.

Most of those who write about the borderline will agree that this person is split between two distinct frames of mind which, to simplify, we could term "positive" and "negative". Typically this person might talk in an idealizing way about a colleague, only to speak of them on another day in highly critical and aggressive terms. This might be considered simply as ambivalence – after all, we do tend to express positive and negative views of other people – but what distinguishes borderline selves is a complete unawareness that they are holding these opposing views. What clinicians had discovered was a permanent split in the self, such that the two prominent domains (the positive and the negative) seemed to have no communication with one another.

Some clinicians, myself included, think this diagnosis was overestimated and applied too indiscriminately. Many people exhibit some borderline features: hysterics, for example, are perfectly capable of performing borderline splitting if that is what they think their good psychiatrist wishes to see. Indeed, sceptics joke that the term might be better applied to the clinicians, on the borderline between clarity and confusion about these newfound selves and vacillating over how to approach the challenges of working with them.

That said, however, the person described is distinct both for the split – if one does witness it, it is unforgettable and compelling – and for the intensity of the rage that follows what can seem like a dreamy idealization of self and others. We can see that this diagnosis, arriving in the wake of World War Two and in the midst of the Korean War, may represent on an individual level something endemic to group life, indeed to the life of a nation. If we look back over several hundred years of European history, we can see a clear pattern of countries admiring or hating one another depending on the shifting geopolitical situation. And in 1951, only a few years after Roosevelt and Uncle Joe Stalin had been friends in arms, with the majority of Americans having positive feelings towards the Soviet Union, the two countries flipped and found themselves in states of fear and hatred towards one another.

As we have seen, amongst Europeans and Americans the century before the Great War was a period of unparalleled self-idealization, and romances of infinite conquest, wealth and progress. The devastations of the wars would have brought such high expectations to a dead halt, leaving people in a state of mourning that turned into melancholia. As selves looked to their devastated countries, and to their own lives, they were left in unconscious rage against the lost idealized beliefs that had seemed to promise so much.

Given the history of splitting the object – Britons could admire Germans in one era and then hate them in another – European thought, occurring at the level of the nation state, was predicated on the necessity of splitting; realpolitik mandated affection if it was in the interests of the nation, and enmity if it was not. This institutionalized splitting, which became a part of social logic in international relations, trickled down into a paradigm for all human relationships, whether one to one or in groups. All psycho-diagnoses reflect the mentalities of their time, and in the mid-twentieth century a splitting of the self into two radically different positions (extreme optimism, extreme pessimism) points towards an unconscious identification with these two positions within the human personality.

We have seen how, at the beginning of Camus' novel, Meursault was indifferent to the death of his mother; as indifferent as he would appear to be to his murder of the Arab on the beach as well as his subsequent incarceration. This character position moves away from all feelings, which are split off from the self's frame of mind.

Meursault represents the self killed off by the wars; the borderline is that self resurrected, but as a reconstructed being. Whilst Maggie Schlegel pleads that we must "only connect" emotion with language, the borderline is predicated on the opposite: on there being no connection between thought and feeling. Something of a throwback to Stevenson's *Dr Jekyll and Mr Hyde*, in which the self is split into two completely separate characters, the 1950s self was both a happy-go-lucky being and an enraged and embittered soul.

The ferocity with which the borderline swings back and forth between positive and negative attitudes towards the same object brings to mind something of the cyclical character of manic depression. And, as discussed, the manic aspect of the nineteenth century self relied on projecting its depressed sides into others-to-soon-be-victims. But what happens when this strategy fails? What happens when, for example, going to war with those who embody the projected does not result in the type of victory imagined?

One solution would be a permanent split in the self, in which the two parts remain without any knowledge of each other. So, if warring does not solve the need to get rid of one's murderousness (ironically projected into the vanquished who deserved to be killed) then a back-up strategy might be for one part of the self to go to war leaving the other part free to reject any connection with the negative.

If we understand the borderline self as a cultural suggestion – split the self and never the twain shall meet – then it is possible to make sense of the post-war strategy for pushing on with things. The negative side of selves and society could embrace technology and industrialism, especially if these developments could filter into an arms industry that pursued its connection with warlike visions of the world. Meanwhile, the positive sides of selves and society could glide into the future in serene peace, dreaming of new automobiles, the latest ovens and refrigerators, and beach-side holidays.

And keeping in mind the structuralization of conflict, in which the original dynamic unconscious formation of a mental or cultural position develops into an axiom that has lost any link with its origins, the borderline solution will successfully keep apart radical contradictions between ideological positions. Indeed, it is precisely this structure that suited post-war America, which needed to continue to idealize itself as the liberator of the free world whilst at the same time sustaining its war machine for the series of conflicts to follow.

For the individual, however, the borderline split does not work so well. Because of the structuralization of the polarity between positive and negative affects and mental representations, this person is in perpetual conflict. The self is oppressed by its own machinations: bearing the negative and positive towards the same object, with no conscious knowledge of the contradiction, is an exhausting and debili-tating form of mental installation art. Eventually the self finds that it has shoved others away, and cannot understand why so few regard it with affection.

On a national scale, although it should have been obvious that American foreign policy and arrogant cultural positions had been highly offensive to many people through-out the world, post-9/11 there was genuine bewilderment: "Why do so many people hate us?" It seemed that they were unable to correlate the post-war history of American imperialism in South America, the Middle East, South East Asia and beyond with the resulting anti-Americanism.

The split between the ideal America and the paranoid America, between a country of promise and a country of profound prejudice, created a confusing object presentation. There were many around the world who hated America, but who also loved it. A split nation evoked split responses, and the double bind could be oppressive. Some would maintain that the nineteenth century was the era of sexual oppression, and certainly Freud concentrated on its *repression*, and specifically on the censorship of sexual and aggressive ideas that created the repressed unconscious. He showed how derivatives of the repressed would show up in sessions, through the versatile veils of language that disguised buried fantasies and memories, concealing them from censorial consciousness.

At this time – indeed from the previous century – other forms of censorship were gathering mass and structure. This was a censorship organized, not against unacceptable ideas, but against the self's right *to be*. Oppression came in many forms and histories: the poverty of the working class; the subordinating of women and children; the domination of countries by leaders who sent millions to their deaths in the "cumulative trauma"[3] of war after war; the assimilation of human beings into the forces of capitalism that overrode the rights of the individual. Although Freud's view of oppression was initially localized to inner censorship, in *Civilization and Its Discontents*, written after the Great War, he turned to a different conflict: the one between the demands of society and the urges of the self.

Life in a society required that selves regulate their sexual and aggressive drives by transferring some of that energy to the self's conscience. Freud termed this the "superego"; it was a specialized part of the ego that provided the power and authority necessary in order to govern selves in groups. In return for the frustrating loss of uninhibited sexual and aggressive actions, we receive the love and affection of our superego which affords us a different kind of gratification. This is akin to a local civic pride: a type of pleasure gained from being part of a community with other selves who have made the same sacrifice, but who also derive love of the self from a part of the ego.

A problem with the concept of the superego, however, is that one person's idea of the good may be another's vision of evil. An American Republican senator of the twenty-first century may have a conscience which tells him that government must not provide social welfare for its citizens as this will undermine their ability to look after themselves. Those who are so persuaded would look upon the policies of the Democratic Party as sabotaging the prospects of a robust economy – and economic prosperity will be to everyone's good.

No doubt some of the plantation owners of the American South believed that their African American slaves were benefitting from the social structure of the plantation. They would have been genuinely offended by the notion that they were oppressed.

When studying the effects of slavery on the human subject,[4] the distinguished historian Kenneth Stampp argued that slaves feigned various types of incapacity as a form of resistance. When they "accidentally" broke machinery, or appeared too ignorant to follow instructions, they were deliberately committing bungled actions. These were not unconscious indications of a Freudian "return of the repressed"; their pseudo-stupidity[5] was a defence. It was what we might term *the return of the oppressed*.

Frantz Fanon used Freud's concept of overdetermination to focus on the effect of the other's oppression of the self, as opposed to one's own self-censorship.[6] He wrote that he was "overdetermined from the outside",[7] oppressed by actions committed by those in power.

> I came into the world imbued with the will to find a
> meaning in things, my spirit filled with the desire to
> attain to the source of the world, and then I found that
> I was an object in the midst of other objects .... Sealed
> into that crushing objecthood, I turned beseechingly to
> others.[8]

Freud's concept of the role of the superego in the formation of social conscience is profound, but this is the same
superego that deems urges unacceptable and causes their
repression. The repressed refers to specific mental contents
that have been banished from consciousness; the oppressed
refers to human thinking that has been forced to become
suspended or distorted. Whereas a repressed thought can
return to consciousness through the re-routing of ideas, the
oppressed involves an alteration, not in the contents of
the mind, but in its capacities; it compromises the mental
process that would have constructed the thought to begin
with, producing a cumulative degradation of perception,
thinking and communication. The repressed, therefore, re-
sides in the unconscious as the successful work of censorship;
the oppressed is also to be found in the unconscious but as a
failed effort, bearing the trace of what might have been
ideationally created.

And it links up with other experiences of failure. The
cumulative effect of thousands of such failed possibilities
forms a mental network of the mangled – ideas half formed
and left disabled. The history of this sad evolution leaves
the self at a loss, in a state of unconscious grief, enduring
a mourning that, if it goes unrecognized, can be endless.
If driven to express its contents, a self de-formed in this
way would be burdened further with the impossibility of
translating the aggregate of contents into sense-able ideas.

Aspects of the way we communicate and think in the
twenty-first century can be seen as forms of *psychic flight*
from the overwhelming weight of inheriting a world shattered by dumb thoughtlessness. However, from the beginning,
aspects of the psychoanalytical method – the freedom to put
into words ideas formed as the unthought known – have
mitigated the oppressions suffered by analysands. The
care given to the speechless self, exemplified in the works
of Ferenczi, Balint, Winnicott, Khan, Coltart and others,
implicitly recognizes the reality that some people suffer
"overdetermination from the outside". A Freudian analysis
offers a pathway to cure through mitigating the pain of distressing contents and discovering forms for the articulation
of one's being. Both find their way into sentient speech,

contained and sustained by the attentive care of the deeply listening analyst. When the oppressed is returned through psychoanalysis, it is transformed from compromised forms of reception, thought and communication into the ordinary forms by which we live.

We have discussed how one response to the radical changes of the nineteenth century was to get caught up in euphoria and enter a manic frame of mind, one that could release a murderous drive to eliminate the depressed parts of the self that had been projected into victims in waiting. Another solution, seen in Forster's portrayal of Henry Wilcox, was to remove the self from its reflective capacity and to identify with productivity. This heralds the normopathic self we see more clearly in the mid-twentieth century, something we shall discuss in the next chapter.

In manic depression and in the borderline we see a splitting of the self, and we turn now to another split in which one part of the self remains immersed in events whilst another part detaches from them. The *dissociated self* is a formation in personality that seems to have served cultural demands during and after the war in Vietnam.

The borderline split allows no communication between the opposing parts. The dissociative self, on the other hand, is distanced from a traumatized part of the personality, but this is not out of sight – indeed, it is in full view. Unlike the borderline, the dissociated self is walking hand-in-hand with its traumatized other half, like a soldier rescuing a comrade in the field of battle. However, the net effect will be a lack of communication between the two sides; the observing self is strangely indifferent to the self that is wounded.

American innocence had been built upon the house of cards of self-idealization. Vulnerable ultimately to incontestable evidence of its capacity for grievous wrongdoing, the Vietnam era opened a fissure in American identity that has never been healed. The nation would be forever divided between those who believed in the war, and may have fought in Vietnam, and those who refused to take part in what they considered to be a war crime. Not a year goes by without the country glorifying the soldiers who took part in that war;

about the young people who refused to fight on moral grounds there is complete silence.

When a person, group or nation finds an issue too complex or too mentally painful, it may be dealt with by a form of *deferral*. It is as if the unconscious is saying "this cannot be thought of now – it is much too raw – but maybe one day . . .". Given all that had already taken place in the twentieth century, it is hardly surprising, perhaps, that Americans and Europeans had little mental space left to think about Vietnam – about what was done there and at what cost.

However, if the deferred mutates into a permanent refusal to think about an issue as serious as Vietnam, it causes an ongoing fissure in society that will deepen and widen. America had already been divided by the Civil War, and the divisions prompted by Vietnam unconsciously joined forces with the prior fissure. Psychologically speaking, the divided country had never been the united states of America.

Reviewing the deeply divisive election of 2016, the eminent American journalist Carl Bernstein[9] described his country as in the midst of "a cold civil war". The memory of Vietnam – ironically, another country's civil war which the Americans had entered – sustained the split in the American population, resulting in a stand-off between its citizens forty-five years after the war had ended.

A fissure such as this warrants attention in this study because it exemplifies how individual and collective minds are compromised and diminished by conflict. In the case of Vietnam, a country that had seen itself as a "beacon upon a hill" had committed atrocities beyond its imagination. Indeed, the realities of the war were banished from being imagined, and it would never be acknowledged in sustained public discourse how far the American leadership and its military had gone in betraying American ideals. Although its citizens knew the difference between right and wrong, after the psychosis of Vietnam the American mind that had existed before – one capable of experiencing guilt and of reflecting on its mistakes – could not be restored. The failure to "process" the war left a rather remarkable country disabled.

Deferral and the refusal to think about a phenomenon are forms of dissociation. We dissociate from a lived experience when we find it shocking; indeed, dissociation is itself a form of shock. Unlike splitting, when we shove something out of mind and out of sight, the dissociated remains as a cognitive object that is in theory viewable. But if a self remains in shock, that object cannot be properly thought. And if time passes and an entire society makes a decision (however understandable) not to stir things up, this means that the group has protected itself by electing to be remote from the lived.

So dissociation may be a rather effective means of surviving a shocking event, preventing further trauma and protecting the group (or self) from being overwhelmed. But if this is structuralized, then the structure – in this case a collective refusal to process a catastrophic event in a nation's history – becomes a superordinate phenomenon that can, ironically, usurp the damaging effect of the original event. Horror films about the walking dead might be understood, perhaps, as a visual metaphor, both for those killed in action and for those at home for whom a part of the self has died through dissociation.

We can now follow the lineage of fractured selves from the manic depressive and borderline to the dissociative. There is a sequence: hot-headed, full-blooded grandiose action; a splitting of the self into an idealistic part that is able, perhaps, to hold on to good memories, and an enraged, embittered self chewing on the negative; and, finally, the death of the self's soul (Meursault); an empty being walking through the fields of battle (Vietnam) like a ghost coming to the rescue of those who have fallen.

This is the logic of tragedy. Whether it is Sophocles' *Oedipus* or Shakespeare's *King Lear*, the tragic begins with a full-on rash action. It is followed by a split in the protagonists, caused by what has happened, and this is succeeded by the dying-off (or murder) of the remnants of those who were part of the original burst of action. The story ends with an isolated heroic figure – a ghost of what he once was – unable to alter the fateful course of action determined by the blindness of hubris.

Notes

1   See Robert Knight. "Borderline states", *Bulletin of the Menninger Clinic.* January, 1953: (1): 1–12. Knight was not the first psychoanalyst to use this term. In fact, his essay in part addresses those authors in the United Kingdom and the USA who referred to it in a dismissive way. However, it is of interest to our discussion here to note that this was a term bandied around the West that met initially with disapproval in the post-war years. It took time and in particular Knight's position – as Director of the eminent Menninger Clinic in Topeka – to establish itself as a term that would then gain prominence. It was, in effect, a culturally driven diagnosis.

2   See Otto Kernberg. *Borderline Conditions and Pathological Narcissism.* New York, Aronson, 1975.

3   Masud Khan's concept of "cumulative trauma" might serve us well as a theoretical construct to identify the imbrication of oppression in the modern self. See Masud Khan. "The concept of cumulative trauma" in *The Privacy of the Self.* London, Hogarth, 1974 [1963], pp. 42–58.

4   Kenneth M. Stampp. *The Peculiar Institution: Slavery in the Ante-Bellum South.* New York, Vintage, 1956.

5   There are several psychoanalytical essays on pseudo-stupidity. I think that Margaret Mahler's essay on pseudo-imbecility is a masterpiece. See "Pseudoimbecility: A Magic Cap of Invisibility" in Margaret S. Mahler. *The Selected Papers of Margaret S. Mahler. Volume One: Infantile Psychosis and Early Contributions.* New York, Jason Aronson, 1979 [1942], pp. 3–16.

6   For a psychoanalytical study of "mental slavery" see Barbara Fletchman Smith. *Mental Slavery: Psychoanalytical Studies of Caribbean People.* London, Rebus Press, 2000. Also see Nancy Hollander. *Uprooted Minds: Surviving the Politics of Terror in the Americas.* New York, Routledge, 2010. Hollander's book is a fine study of many of the factors that now contribute to widespread mental pain in large parts of our world.

7   See Frantz Fanon. *Black Skin, White Masks.* New York, Grove, 2008 [1952], p. 95.

8   Frantz Fanon. "The Fact of Blackness" in Les Back and John Solomos (eds), *Theories of Race and Racism.* London, Routledge, 2008, p. 257.

9   See Daniel Chaitin. "Carl Bernstein: Cold civil war media embrace 'different truths'". *Washington Examiner* (online), 16 July 2017. http://washingtonexaminer.com/carl-bernstein-cold-civil-war-gripping-us-as-media-embrace-different-truths/article /2628813.

6

Normopathy and the
compound syndrome

America, a nation widely recognized as the "leader of the free world", was failing to lead in the psychological sense; its politicians and its citizens had failed within the human dimension. It was perhaps a relief, therefore, for the country to turn itself over to a caretaker: to market forces and trickle-down economics – a system that would take the place of human leadership.

People were exhausted by a century of conflict that had eviscerated the ideal of pursuing just causes and generating a sense of meaning. Postmodernist philosophers were shelving the problem posed by the crisis of meaning, arguing that, since there was no self anyway, what was there to lose? Although the universities still received their students, churches their flocks, and the *New Yorker* and the *New York Review of Books* retained their readers, there was a gradual but eventually perceptible decline of interest in the humanities and liberal arts. After several hundred years, the church was losing its progressive thinking, and the intelligentsia found themselves no longer capable of forming an avant-garde: of bringing the future into the present in evocatively challenging ways.

By the start of the twenty-first century, Americans and Europeans had turned away in significant numbers from introspective living. Within a decade the country was ingesting prescription medications that helped people tune out of the meanings of anxiety and depression, and lose touch with the ideas embedded in these affects. Seeking a safer and less disturbing day-to-day existence, they turned away from subjectivity. They dropped out of their minds.

This disinterest in inner life allowed another personality formation to develop. In the past I referred to this as the *normotic*. Joyce McDougall called it the *normopath*,[1] a term I now prefer. Unlike the borderline, the normopath seeks refuge from mental life by immersing the self in material comfort and a life of recreation. In the chapters to follow, we shall see how this personality evolved through acts of identification with the machinery of globalization. This was not a new idiom in personality – I discuss how Henry Wilcox in E.M. Forster's novel *Howards End* is a portrait of the normopath, but by the third quarter of the twentieth century normopathic life was on the rise.

In 1971, Winnicott[2] stated that there was an opposite to the withdrawn, schizoid personality often encountered by psychoanalysts: "one would have to state that there are others who are so firmly anchored in objectively perceived reality that they are ill in the opposite direction of being out of touch with the subjective world and with the creative approach to fact" (1971, p. 78). Winnicott noted this formation but sadly, at this point, a year before his death, he could only sketch it as a theory of a personality.

In the late 1970s and early 1980s, during spells of work in the new communities of Orange County, California, southern Arizona and parts of Texas, I was surprised by the number of young people I encountered who had experienced sudden breakdowns or had attempted suicide, with few signs of distress prior to these events. It seemed they lived in a culture in which parents, family, friends, educators and even clinicians seemed oblivious to the existence of internal mental life. I wrote:

> A normotic person is someone who is abnormally normal. He is too stable, secure, comfortable and socially extrovert. He is fundamentally disinterested in subjective life and he is inclined to reflect on the thingness of objects, on their material reality, or on 'data' that relates to material phenomena.

(88)[3]

I noted that their fundamental characteristic was a lack of interest in subjective life, and that "such a person appears genuinely naïve if asked to comment on issues that require either looking into oneself or the other in any depth" (88).

This naivety was striking. Unlike the borderline, the normopath was not filled with anger or rancour but was seemingly quite content. Unlike the manic depressive, s/he was not driven to invent her or his own fantasied, or mytho-poetic universe. Indeed, the normopath loves facts. I wrote:

> He does not have a passion for factual data in order to establish a common knowledge that sponsors a group's creativity . . . facts are collected and stored because this activity is reassuring. It is part of a personal evolution in which he unconsciously attempts to become an object in the object world.
>
> (89)

This inclination, to become an object in the object world – alongside motorbikes or boats or nifty tennis shoes – appeared before the age of the internet and the machinery of IT. The normopathic self is, then, a precursor to what I shall later refer to as the *transmissive self*. Both seek refuge through acts of identification with the material world in which they live.

There was an anguish within many clinicians who were working with normopathic people in the 1970s and 1980s that bears on our interest in meaning and melancholia. In fact they themselves would sometimes display what seemed like normopathic reactions; their rather cheery, hearty responses to tragic events were attempts to skim over the traumatic sides of life and avoid their own vulnerability. I described the normopathic life as follows:

> From the supermarket to the pet shop; from the sportsware store to the large hardware shop: from a lunch with friends in which there is an itemization of actions lived out by each, to the home for a listless cleansing of the kitchen; from a tennis match to the Jacuzzi: this person can live a life without ever blinking

an eye. If his mother or father is dying the normotic does not feel grief, but instead engages in a detailed examination of the nature of the disease, the technology of the hospital treating the person and the articulation of clichés that are meant to launder the experience of death: "Well, she's very old you know, and we've all got to go some time."

(90)

In the essay I recounted my experience of interviewing an adolescent, "Tom", who had attempted suicide after fumbling a ball during a high-school football game. I discovered in the course of the meeting that his family had just moved to that area, a long way from his home of origin, but that neither he nor the family thought this was a big deal. I focused on how Tom's lack of interest in matters of the heart and the mind seemed to be evidence of a personality that "admitted of no inquiry or reflection" (97).

Looking back now, thirty years later, I am struck by what I did not write. By the end of the interview, which was held as part of a hospital "grand round", I was feeling deeply moved; indeed, close to tears. So too were many others in the room although, notably, some of the staff were as removed from affect as Tom himself. What hit me so forcefully was how lost he seemed and how uncared for, even though it was very clear that his parents, siblings and friends were sincere and loving people in their own way.

So why did I omit this most important emotional fact from my account? Why not state the obvious – that this young man's suicide attempt was so deeply sad because he knew of no way that he or anyone else could help him? It was his utter *aloneness* that was heartbreaking.

As we shall see, although many young people in the second decade of the twenty-first century share some characteristics with Tom, what is noteworthy is that they no longer seem to evoke a sense of grief or mourning within the clinical community. Instead, in their android-like enthusiasm for their app world, imbued with an arrogant sense of privileged access, if anything we tend to find them off-putting. What Tom unknowingly communicated to myself and others was that the adjustments made by normopathic selves were forms of grief stored within the self. My inability to bring it into my consciousness, and thus to write about it, echoed Tom's own incapacity.

Some parts of the normopathic society have formed themselves into a type of counterculture: people have retreated into gated communities – some metaphorically, and some in reality. (Interestingly, Tom's family lived in one of these communities.) In the 1950s there were only a few such developments, but by the 1980s they had multiplied, with some adopting romantic identities. "Cape Cod Village" seemed like rather an anomaly since this was California not Massachusetts, but then Disneyland, a gated theme park offering pre-packaged joy, was only twenty miles away.

By the turn of the century, around 1 per cent of the American population had withdrawn into these compounds, and were living largely removed from contact with ordinary people in the outside world. The lords of the manor of the medieval era may be said to have done much the same, but in fact their villages were populated by peasants and there was a close symbiotic relation between the lord and his serfs.

Even outside their compounds, the oligarchs of the twenty-first century were insulated from real life as they sat in their limousines with tinted windows, escorted from one bubble to another. No need to use a commercial aircraft to reach a private island hideaway when one can travel by private jet and be greeted at one's destination by more tinted windows.

Although the rest of the population came nowhere near this standard of luxury, the ethos of life in the compound spread insidiously across the upper middle class. It was no longer necessary to visit retail outlets; now anything people desired for material comfort could be simply ordered and delivered. Professionals would provide in-home visits: there was rarely a need to venture into the outside world. When people dined out or visited the theatre or cinema, they remained inside an unconscious envelope derived from the compound culture. They walked amongst the ordinary folks of their cities like tourists who found the lives of the locals "interesting" or "amusing" or "sad"; a sort of moral compensation for dissociated indifference.

In time, however, some of these compound selves began to suffer from a paradoxical internal situation: they had everything, yet it gave them little. Psychoanalysts might sometimes be sought out, but usually only after various more fashionable forms of therapy had been tried. The sorts of comments made by analysts were outside their experience, and would often lead to a startled response: "Do you always say things like that to the people you see?"

"Compound syndrome", as I shall name it, involves a form of deprivation that creates a sensorially and intellectually undernourished self. People may adapt to this loss with further withdrawal from the world of stimulation – that is, from anything deriving from the outside world that impacts on the self. After being guided and provided for by others for decades, people become less capable of astute judgement, less able to differentiate one issue from another, and less skilled in providing ordinary self-guidance. In other words, they have lost essential capabilities.

In the absence of sufficient stimulating and novel experiences, the self gradually loses interest in seeking the spice of life because it cannot remember what this felt like. With nothing enriching to recall, memory itself becomes atrophied; with loss of memory other intellectual capacities dwindle, and eventually there arrives a new matrix of existential psychic positions: a general impoverishment of the ego that is accompanied by a deep and widespread depression. Their fellow compound selves may serve as a group that provides mutual admiration, but with the lack of fresh blood and fresh thinking, in the end the euphorias of success and glitter wear off. Although still surrounded by conspicuous wealth and provision, these now serve to objectify their alienation.

Many compound selves turn to alcohol, prescription medication or recreational drugs, seeking relief through the jolting effect of intoxication or a trip into a past in which they felt alive. They are often provided for in "rehab" centres, high-end establishments that are in themselves isolating compounds. These tend to offer life coaches who inject their clients with a manic boost – ex-Navy SEALs or Army Rangers lead their flock in para-military psychological ventures – or be staffed with ex-users who convey a tough love.

This will work for some; they may be rebooted into the selves they were before the depression hit. Although they may not have gained much insight, they may manage to move out of the compound and back into the real world. But the majority of clients will return to their enclaves, moving from therapist to rehab and back again, quietly returning to the folded arms of their significant others.

When psychoanalysis succeeds with people who suffer from compound syndrome, this seems to be because the patient has responded to the uniquely challenging intellectual acumen of this form of thinking. The psychoanalytic process *in itself* has been a novel and stimulating experience. At long last the self has something to think about.

Along with the borderline, the dissociated and the normopath, compound syndrome selves came into existence within a society that had suffered radical internal loss. The world no longer found it meaningful to search for meaning. Compound selves, living in the aspic of their protected surroundings, may not seem deserving of our compassion: they often appear indifferent to the suffering of those around them. However, what we are noting here is a deterioration in the mental functioning and empathic capabilities of a privileged group of individuals, many of whom are in positions of power and influence in our lives. And this should be of concern to us all.

Notes

1   See Joyce McDougall. *Plea for a Measure of Abnormality*. New York, International Universities Press, 1980 [1978].
2   See D.W. Winnicott. *Playing and Reality*. London, Penguin, 1980 [1971].
3   See Christopher Bollas. "Normotic illness" in *The Shadow of the Object: Psychoanalysis of the Unthought Known*. London, Routledge, 2017 [1987], pp. 87–102.

7

Transmissive selves[1]

The Rose Café, in Venice, California, is a near perfect place to meet up for lunch. The food is great and people from all walks of life gather under an outdoor canopy to be caressed by the sea breeze coming off the great Pacific Ocean.

In the spring of 2012 I got together there with a group of people whom I knew a bit and I was stunned at what struck me as a sea change in lunch society. There were about eight of us, and people arrived gradually in pairs and singles. Some did not greet us at first as they were deep into their phones, largely unaware of the actual world; others at the table were smiling softly at their groins, reading their text messages.

This was not a group of nouveaux introverts at some kind of convention. The phones were enthusiastically passed around: photos of an event attended by some of those present were met with the usual exclamations – "wow", "cool".

When we were all seated, and after the waiter had tried visiting the table three or four times, I came out of my psychic carapace and said: "So, shall we order?" A glass of water was knocked over, bags dropped, alarmed heads popped up: I had verbally barged in on what in another era might have been a seance.

Each generation finds its inheritors' transformations disturbing. Confucius mourned the passing of the Golden Age and found modern trends in Chinese society so distressing that *The Analects* could be viewed as a literature of reproach. As the opening sentence in "The Thing",[2] Heidegger writes "All distances in space and time are shrinking" (165).

He argues that although television and modern media seem to have brought the world closer together, in fact such immediacy has created a disguised form of distance; we are not closer, but further apart: "Everything gets lumped together into uniform distanceless" (166). We lose contact with the thingness of the world. The cure? To be with things – "the thing things" and "thinging gathers" (174). "Thinging", he concludes, "is the nearing of the world" (181). Things reverberate through us, and nourish us. (Heidegger could have scripted a convincing credo for the normopathic solution.)

When we think of "globalization", a cluster of ideas comes to mind that is an amalgam of curiously conjoined images, as if the word enacts itself. Even as we try to come up with a precise definition, the term seems to become globalized: it means many things to many people.

We cannot escape this collective enactment, which immediately places us into the global community; like it or not – and many do not – we are automatically membered into being "globals". Whether we live in rural Mississippi (where the unaffordability of landlines makes cell phones mandatory), in Perth, or New York, or a small village in Kenya, most people are now connected to one another. Google is not merely a search engine, it is an "aka" for "global community". We may wonder if we have ever before walked so blindly into a mass social transformation, from so many different directions, so many diverse backgrounds, and with so little idea of where we are going.

Shortly I shall turn to a narrow and limited reading of globalization, one that will focus on the mobile selves of this world, discussed by Elliott and Urry in their passionate and brilliant book *Mobile Lives*.[3] The world, they argue, is now divided between those who are genuinely mobile – an elite who have create a new economy of "network capital" and are part of a "mobility field" in which "meetingness" takes place – and those others (most of the world) who are still locals, fixed to the spot and less able to take part in the vital formation of social networking, even if they have the technical means to access such a network.

I think their argument is compelling. The reality is that with "globalization" we are embracing a term that has few precedents in our lexicon. It might be considered part of the family of "internationalism" – a word that hails from the early nineteenth century and might be thought of as its predecessor. Internationalism recognized the diversity of the world and the inevitability that nations will engage one another, especially through trade. But like internationalism, the term "globalization" has become so overused and exploited, especially to advance the free movement of capital around the world, that it has become something of a synonym for "clandestine movement across borders". The grain trade and the drug trade are both globalized forms of profit from cross-border communications.

Heidegger's wariness speaks to an aspect of a lengthy transformation of human being into mediated interrelatedness that began with the printed word. There has always been anxiety lest such mediations separate us from some more primal experience of the real. Indeed, memory itself is, arguably, a mediation: we call up the thing in various forms of the imaginary. Wordsworth's definition of the power of poetry – "emotion recollected in tranquility" – implicitly argues that Grasmere exists, not in the momentous grasp of the real, but in the self's recollection of it when separated from it, later on.

In fact we live in multiple worlds. We walk about in the real and have direct experiences of things which may be highly evocative, but then we walk down memory lane and see these things in a different way. Although from one point of view we exist in the unrepresentable private world of the self's inner life, we also live amongst others: first in the thing we call a family, then in a society, in a nation, and now we find ourselves living in the global community. We are many things to many people; and increasingly our "I" has many "me's".[4]

As the world changes so do we.

But how different are we in the era of globalization? In attempting to map the psychological territory, it is helpful to divide relationships now being lived into the "actual" and the "virtual"; those relations we are having in real time with actual living people versus those we are having in cyberspace.

Take the Rose Café. Whereas in the past eight people lunching were just eight people lunching, now along with the actuals there are a number of virtuals in the equation.

Each person has a phone or an iPad, and as they talk to one another they also receive phone calls, emails and text messages that temporarily remove them from those physically present in order to communicate with absent others. Actuals give way to virtuals. Sometimes one group member might even text another, creating a simultaneous parallel virtual reality to their actual spatial relation. And of course all the actuals in their social network will on occasion become virtuals.

Not so long ago, such a group might have been offended if one of their number glanced at a laptop, texted or engaged in a phone conversation, but in our new age people seem to have adjusted to this sort of dining scene, unless by consent they decide to turn themselves off. On that occasion I found myself out of it because I did not have an absent companion; I was not open to an invitation from a virtual.

"Multitasking" – a relatively new word – has become a virtue. Our *operant* capacities – including our ability to perform several functions at the same time – have become not only admirable but essential. Indeed, they are part of the function of social networking. Whilst in the past we could simply sit and watch television or talk on the phone – leaving it to the technological object to function for us – we have now become part of the function of the world.

I refer to this new self-formation as *transmissive*. We use all kinds of objects that transmit information, from old and familiar ones such as the printed word, radio, television and telephone, to the many new forms of social connectedness via the internet. Facebook, Instagram and Twitter allow us to become, so to speak, part of the show. But it is not simply that we are now visible: as we transmit our private selves to the world, we also become a function in that new order.

We distinguish, then, between our substantive self, a content that we transmit to others, and our formative self, who is the communicator, the vehicle of such dissemination.

We may not like to think of ourselves as equivalent to iPads, smartphones and the like, but we have become extensions of these objects as much as they are extensions of us. In this respect we are now vital parts of the form-world of transmissive devices: indeed, when we upgrade these devices we also upgrade ourselves.

In the early years of this century, if I was invited to visit a retail outlet to purchase one or other of these new devices I almost always said no. I felt repulsed by the idea of walking into an android factory for a part replacement. I developed a kind of neurotic symptom: for no obvious reason, if the radio or TV was on I would automatically turn it off.

"Hey, I was watching that!"

"But you are on your computer and texting someone with your phone."

"So what? I can walk and chew gum at the same time! Turn it back on!"

Although I learnt to become rather more careful about disconnecting transmissive objects, I must confess to a quiet satisfaction in being something of a counter-revolutionary, making a small protest against the inanities of the new world. But in truth I too was adapting. To keep up with the transmissive object world we must all become "techies", able to operate all the latest products. I had to learn how to be a functionary within that order: to accommodate a new version of my self.

We have our functions – as farmers, fishermen, builders, teachers – and our work is defined, in part, by the historical identity of any "pro-fession". Function sculpts form, and the way we live has been largely destined by our vocation. So a farmer lives his or her life according to the seasons, planning crop selection, placement and planting, and deciding when to harvest according to the weather. A teacher has to operate according to the scheduled lessons expected by the school, considering when and how to introduce which subjects, when to allocate time to the individual student and when to the group as whole. The form of a teacher's year will follow the multiple functions of teaching.

The question is, how much do we identify with our functions? When a farmer farms or a teacher teaches, to what

extent do these functions dictate the self; its inner organization and its emanations? On the whole I believe that
people would not wish to be defined wholly by their work.
They perform these functions but their selves are not to be
equated with them.

Sometimes, by that common and ancient act we term
"hysteria", people do temporarily cross over; what they are
doing takes over the self for a while. Kids coming out of
a scary movie may identify with the monster in the film
and try to freak each other out. Identifications of this kind,
especially in a group, can reverse anxiety from the passive to
the active position and transfer private terror into a group
process that detoxifies things. In order to overcome their
fears they act out what they have endured, but such mimetic
representations of the shocking will be transitory and soon
identification gives way to memory.

However, the globalized world, at least as it is being
marketed, seems to demand something more than simple
mastery of the newly changing objects of transmission. It
seems we are being asked to assume a role as part of the
function of the network, indeed, to identify with it in order to
reverse our initial passive position into an active one. If the
constant presentation of new transmissive objects makes us
anxious, one solution is to reverse the anxiety proactively, by
eagerly awaiting the new transmissive object so that we can
be "ahead of the game". Indeed, if our next role is announced
to us some months ahead of time, with the prospect of new
technological inventions already providing a heads-up as to
expected functional changes, we can be in role as soon as the
commodity appears. As the new device rolls off the production
line and the queue of consumers waits to grab it, transmissive
objects and transmissive selves meet up.

The tasks of farmers and teachers require different
frames of reference, different forms of intelligence, and they
may be said to have differing mentalities specific to their
vocations. A person's mentality consists, to some extent, in
the particular types of intelligence they bring to bear on the
way they perceive, organize and communicate their specific
lived experience.

What are we to make, then, of the "global self" – less a vocation in waiting, more a necessity imposing itself upon us – in which the commodified transmissive objects unify us as common transmitters across the entire globe? The farmer or teacher in any city or village in the world is invited now into a community of fellow practitioners, who are not simply passively participant in a new form of media but are actively transmissive, playing their part in the function of the object world.

The upsides of this new world order are obvious, but as with any radical change, especially if it is worldwide, time might be well spent mulling over the downsides. As discussed, in the early twentieth century and especially in the Great War, group psychology eclipsed the individual self. When any large group begins to trumpet a new age with new visions, and the world starts to change, it is time to think about what kinds of selves we are becoming. In our era, the disparity between degrees of access to new forms of technology creates a widening gap between those who are employing these prosthetic extensions of the self and those who are not, and are thus potentially disabled.

Let's return once more to the Rose Café.

The group of diners are talking about the developments in Egypt that led to the ousting of Mubarak. These events have been extensively reported on the TV news and covered in all the mass media – indeed, Facebook, Twitter, email and so forth have played an important part in the revolution itself. Jill, Jake, Martha and Tony are discussing the situation. Martha is mid-sentence on how brave she thought the demonstrators were, when she gets a phone call; Jake takes over where Martha left off, but then he gets a text message so Jill steps in; Martha is back – they continue to talk about Egypt for the next twenty minutes with people dropping in and out of the conversation here and there as they each touch base with absent virtuals.

The discussion happens in fragments of narrative, each of which can be dropped by one speaker and picked up by another – speakers become interchangeable. There is a rule to this discourse: no topic should be so significant as to preclude anyone dropping out to talk to virtuals. Conversation must be shallow enough to be disposable, a fast food-for-thought that can be gobbled up and discarded by moving from one topic to another.

The ease with which groups of people can do this is impressive – talk suspended entirely if everyone happens to be otherwise engaged – and for a while they can look like a group of strangers sharing a table, before they re-animate as actuals and come back into space and time together. They have just been away for a while, fulfilling tasks in the social network of virtual reality.

In many ways, in the course of a day, we associate with one another, but when we abandon actuals to talk to virtuals we are momentarily dissociated. If everyone present is engaged in talking to a virtual, the group is in a state of mutual dissociation. This is an important function of the new world: we split the self into the associating self and the dissociating self, and a new function of the group is to tolerate both states as they emanate from each person. Indeed, the days of people-watching, sitting on a subway or strolling down an esplanade are dwindling. Fellow subway travellers become dissociates, each plugged in to a private technology. Interchangeable discourse is ideal for the transmission of information. As transmissive selves, our obligation is simply to pass on what we have seen or heard, mimicking the function of the transmitting objects: transmissive discourse is information (of one kind or another) passed on without reflection, analysis or any discernibly unique interest to the self.

The previous chapter discussed how people and societies can dissociate themselves from the emotional issues resident within personal or social conflict; by detaching the self from the conflict it can be observed from afar, as if we are not part of it. This chapter has looked at a step further down the road: selves are wired to adapt to the global community as distant participants. Dissociation now *precedes* acts of engagement because decades of dissociative activity have become part of an adaptive mental structure.

The internet allows psychically systemic[5] flight from the actual, as we live in a virtual reality with varied avatars of the self; our doppelgängers allow us to speak through alternate personalities permitting engagement with one another online. Yet although Facebook seems to display a transparent self, what is offered are mere photo snaps of engagement in the actual world.

And what is passed on to our children?

Danah Boyd[6] writes that teenagers' use of social media is driven not by desire but by oppression. Anxious parents no longer want their children playing on the streets of America, and Boyd notes in her travels that contemporary children do not physically, spontaneously play with one another. Indeed, their parents set up so many scheduled activities that they rarely have a chance to socialize at all except via the internet. Perhaps, then, the development of a virtual self engaged in quick, shallow speech (the abbreviated language of texting, the use of emoticons, tweeting limited to 140 characters a shot) is a compromise between transparency and absolute silence. Cryptic speech keeps people in touch with one another, but not close; we reveal nothing about the privacy of the self – some even go by fictional names – and we engage with little from the other.

As we learn to behave differently, it is not surprising that selves undergo a formal change. A glance into our android future promises, not depth of communication, but a vision from the mental shallows.

Notes

1 An earlier version of this chapter was published as "The transmissive self and transmissive objects in the age of globalization" in Susana Araujo, Marta Pinto and Sandra Bettencourt (eds), *Fear and Fantasy in a Global World*. Leiden, Rodopi/Brill, 2015. I am grateful to the press and the editors for permission to publish the essay in altered form here.

2 Martin Heidegger, "The Thing" in *Poetry, Language, Thought*. New York, Harper & Row, 1971, pp. 165–82.

3 Anthony Elliott and John Urry, *Mobile Lives*. London, Routledge, 2010.

4 The "I"–"me" relation is the structure of internal dialogue between a speaking part of the self, the "I", and a listening part of the self, the "me".

5   It is "psychically systemic" when selves turn to the internet
    without thinking, using it for hours a day, so that it is now part
    of the fabric of one's being.
6   See Danah Boyd. *It's Complicated: The Social Life of Networked
    Teens*. New Haven, CT, Yale University Press, 2014. This book is
    an invaluable resource in understanding the many myths about
    contemporary youth's use of the social network.

8

New forms of thinking

We have examined how early twenty-first-century psychic values are based less on immediate experiences and more on those indirect perceptions spawned by the information revolution. Contemporary selves live several steps removed from engagements in the real, retreating from the anxiety of the unmediated to seek sanctuary in technology that promises a reliable, comfortable, anodyne environment.

Unlike the commitment to modernism so prevalent a century ago, we are now witnessing a cultivated detachment. Instead of the hustle and bustle of city life – in Paris, Berlin, Prague, New York – of the early twentieth century, when artists, poets and intellectuals clashed, enjoyably and of necessity, in order to sharpen their edge, their equivalents in the twenty-first century have retreated into enclaves. The magazines that celebrated dissent have mostly disappeared, cafes that were magnets for intellectual exploration turned into kick-start stopovers for joggers, the flamboyance of new ideas replaced by a generation devoted to "chilling out".

Instead of debate, we have transmission and concession to our role as a part of the machinery of this age.

This move into psychic or environmental enclaves can be understood, at least in part, as an attempt to slow down the near overwhelming speed of the lived. But retreat is not possible because we have changed temporality and spatiality to the point where no one can truly live within it.

The pace of the twenty-first century prohibits sanctuary. In *Cosmopolis*[1] DeLillo writes: "The speed is the point. We are not witnessing the flow of information so much as pure spectacle, or information made sacred, ritually unreadable" (80). How can one chill out within such a fast-moving chain of events? And where will one find those private spaces, traditionally so important in the West, that were formerly sought through spells of time dwelling in literature or music, or in religious or academic pursuits?

In his brilliant if disturbing work *Mindless: Why Smarter Machines Are Making Dumber Humans*[2] Simon Head traces and dissects the disseminative influence of "computer business systems" (CBSs) on workers in almost all areas of the "managed" world: manufacturing, the service industry, the financial sector and elsewhere. As CBSs program workers to speed up their productivity rate by means of minute-by-minute instructions throughout the day, individual judgement is systematically replaced by manuals that tell people how to behave and what to say.

Head writes: "there is an unrelenting emphasis on the need for speed in the execution of processes" (25); "The human element is completely absent in this perfecting of process" (26). DeLillo writes: "People in free societies don't have to fear the pathology of the state. We create our own frenzy, our own mass convulsions, driven by thinking machines that we have no final authority over" (85).

With our customary occupations of time and space foreclosed, we are invited instead to join the streams of IT and AI, which promise to guide us through the spaces and the paces of this "brave new world". The twenty-first-century self is thus programmed into what we may term the *Fastnet*[3] *world*, one that mandates speed at the expense of reflection and judgement. Part of Head's argument is that as systems become more powerful and more ubiquitous, humans become "dumber" because human thought slows down their efficiency. The mentality generated by CBSs promises to the population rapid, ready-made, pre-existent solutions.

For people working in the world of mental health, this demand for quick-fix assurances has not snuck up unnoticed. For decades, insurance companies, health maintenance organizations, national health services and other "providers" have sought briefer forms of psychotherapy than the one delivered by psychoanalysis. To some extent psychoanalysts have adjusted to this, but the trends towards the quick fix have sponsored an assumption that the challenges of mental life (the form of a symptom, the dense thickets of moods, the issues generated by one's past and personality) are best remedied by interventions that will remove the effects of troublesome issues.

This comes with a new axiom: the solution to the problem of mental life is a programme that provides action guidance, and clinicians must offer evidentially effective forms of treatment. What message will the patient take from the session that will help him improve his life? Which comments by the analyst will prove to be most operationally effective? Insurance companies want to know, governments investing money in mental health want to know, and patients, caught up in the rush to solve problems, *expect* to know – and to know quickly.

In many analysands, analysts are observing a shift away from the merit of the unknowable productiveness of unconscious thinking towards the value of knowable remedies that can be put into effect immediately. This type of operational thinking seeks cognitive analogues to the ingestion of medication that will be immediately effective. It sponsors the inclination to develop action statements over reflection.

The analysand who is in this frame of mind will tend to receive an interpretation, not as part of a sequelae of conscious discontinuities connected by unconscious processes, but as a free-standing sound bite, an instruction for altering the behaviour of the self.

So one effect of operationalism[4] is the inclination to develop action statements over reflection. A clinical sample:

"Okay, I get it. So all I have to do now is . . . "[5]
"I notice that you seem to take what I say as a set of instructions for how you can improve yourself."
"Well that's the point, isn't it?"
"It might seem so, but by immediately putting it into a plan for behaviour change, I wonder if you have actually given yourself any time to think about it."

If the patient can understand this interpretation of the formal aspect of the analysis, it may then be possible to discuss ancillary dimensions. There may be a feeling that s/he does not have time to give matters any thought because s/he must come up with an urgent solution to her or his problems. There may be an unconscious fantasy that the mind is a trouble-making entity that needs formulaic structuring in order to be controllable.

In this new utilitarian climate, we witness the emerging of a soft nihilism in which the human subject, and the complex processes of human thought, are implicitly viewed as an impediment to the successful implementation of programmes that are still person dependent. The process of exploring the internal world and using reflective thought to unravel unconscious conflicts is clearly too slow – it may even be a hindrance. What proposes itself as a problem-solving era is increasingly devoted to the trimming down of the human dimension.

These shifts have led, too, to another subtle but profound alteration in the form of human thinking. Our species has always tended to doubt the validity of any prevailing world view, but in the past there has been an assumption that there exists some form of vertical (or hierarchical) cosmology that accords one thing more importance than another. Belief in one's God, for example, would have been put higher on the list of significance than, say, belief in what the weather would be the following week. Whether right or wrong in their beliefs or priorities, for thousands of years people have established these vertical structures of meaning.

In the twenty-first century, however, we see a new form of thought emerging: *horizontalism*.[6] This is the eradication of prioritization in favour of equivalencies that render all ideas equally valid. A sample of horizontalism:

"You seem to cope with your envy of your friend by making yourself indispensable to him."

"Oh. . .YEAH! Yeah. . .and I'm also doing too much biking and stuff like that."

Horizontalism does not recognize a hierarchical order; all ideas are equal and no one thing is intrinsically more important than another. In the Fastnet world, transmissive selves will often be oblivious to the weight of meaning of an object of communication. We may see this on cable news, for example, where a series of fires in the United States, or an impending hurricane, will be given the same air time as a revolution in the Ukraine or a genocide in Africa. The recognized value of the opinions of experienced journalists, scholars and writers is fading as the social democracy of the internet turns us all into experts on any topic. And while this democratization may be healthy in some respects, the downside is the inadvertent promotion of the power of the uninformed self.

When vertical thinking is destroyed and horizontal thought prevails, then difference becomes meaningless. Indeed, differentiation is predicated on the ability to evaluate and to discriminate between objects; to find in alterity a tensional creativity. Difference generates oppositions that will be valued if heterogeneity is assumed to be worthy. But the process of globalization promotes global-selves, uniform beings. This fiction – it could never be a reality – functions as a psychic soporific for homogenized humans. So to operationalism and horizontalism we add *homogenization*: the need to eradicate difference and fashion a world of indistinguishable beings. Unconscious promotion of homogeneity reduces the time taken up with considering different points of view and the resulting tensions. It makes us more efficient and therefore more productive.

In the late nineteenth and early twentieth centuries, modernism might seem to have promoted homogenized living, but the rapid movement of people and ideas and the interweaving discord of differences – in the wake of romanticism, realism, naturalism and imagism – resulted in a convergence of views that was procreative: people came together in order to differ!

In the capital cities of Europe people went to cafes for lively debate, not simply for a shot of coffee. Not so in today's Starbucks world.

And this change is evidenced in the clinical world by a lessening in patients' capacity for "resistance". In psychoanalytic patients, homogenization takes the form of a fear of being perceived as different: "But doesn't everyone think like this?" The Fastnet makes identification and fusion with others so easily accomplished that people assume they will be "on the same page". As they share the same popular cultural experiences, this promotes the sense of being part of a collective norm.

Which brings us to the difference between sight and insight. Some observers consider this the era of "the spectacle"[7] – we seem drawn to the sights of life in the technologically mediated universe. But although we may be sightfully informed, with memories of what we have seen, we have comparatively little insight. Insight involves our consciousness being directed towards the internal world, and it implies interest in the various meanings of our lived experience.

Contemporary selves who post "selfies" on Facebook are asking "What do you see when you see me?" But "selfies", sadly, are in fact no such thing. What they reveal, is not the self but an "other" in a solitary act of estranged intimacy. We take our photo from some distance, as if we were in good company. The selfie equivalents in the nineteenth and twentieth centuries were works of self-examination; realizations of what was taking place within the self. They implied an intimate conversation between the I and the me. This has been a continuous thread of connection with inner life that we can trace back to the sixteenth century, part of an evolution without which the discovery of psychoanalysis would not have been possible.

Many of today's analysands seem disposed to view the self through the lens of the other, as if selfies are a feature of psychotherapy. A patient expects to see into the self through the analyst's interpretation, and s/he assumes that this is the function of the analyst. He is meant to produce an intellectual commodity of thought called "an insight"; the patient is now "the consumer".

When a patient says "I remember you saying that a few weeks ago", s/he is unconsciously demonstrating that what s/he has taken to be an insight is in fact no such thing. It is merely "a sight into the self" created by the analyst's interpretation. Although it has been recollected, it has no

meaning and is likely to have no lasting effect. So the psycho-
therapies face a new challenge: the self is becoming a mere
spectacle in a universe of observable objects. Seeing may be
believing, but is it knowing?

Let us call the use of sight to avoid insight *sightophilia*.
A person who is drawn to seeing rather than thinking is a
sightophile.

One feature of sightophilia is *refractive thinking*. When
an object is met with refractive thought, there is an instan-
taneous emissive ejection of any resulting lines of thought,
away from the subject and into space. Refraction casts
thought onto objects, but these will serve, not as containers
for thoughts that would be retrievable through memory,
but as conduits for dispersing a thought so its contents
will disappear. Refractive thinking selects a minor feature
of a communication and highlights it, sending the core
communication to oblivion. It therefore eliminates meaning.

I say to an analysand:

> "I think your being indispensable to your friend allows
> you to covertly attach yourself to her."
> "You got it. I am indispensable, and I should
> probably watch that. That's brilliant – thanks so much."
> "You seem to have grasped this thought so quickly
> that I'm not sure we have had a chance to think it."
> "Oh, no, I mean it was great. Am I . . . am
> I . . . supposed to think about it?"[8]

In this way, the psychoanalyst is morphed from a companion in exploration into a sage, appreciated in much the
same way as one might be grateful for a good auto mechanic
or computer expert. In place of insight we have sight – albeit
analytically informed sight; in place of reflective thought, we
have refractive thinking and operational imperatives; in
place of carefully constructed vertices of meaning specific to
the psychic and lived history of a subject, we have a homogenized being, dynamically amalgamated (and updated) by
horizontal objects of thought.

"Because time is a corporate asset now", writes DeLillo,
"it belongs to the free market system. The present is harder

to find. It is being sucked out of the world to make way for the future of uncontrolled markets and huge investment potential. The future becomes insistent" (79).

Are the new dimensions of thinking I have explored here forms of efficiency embedded in assumptions about being and relating? Or might we understand them as intermediate adaptations to a changing world in which thinking has been sucked out of the present and referred to the future? Are we now thinking by not thinking? Rather like the pseudo-stupidity of enslaved people, discussed in Chapter 5, it may be that operationalism, horizontalism, homogenization, refraction and sightophilia are transiently adaptive moves adopted to control the bewildering.

Following Badiou, Jameson[9] and others, it seems reasonable to wonder whether suspension of thought and engagement – a form of psychic retreat[10] – is evidence of a dawning *subjecticide*. Less than fifteen years separate Heidegger's question "Why is there being rather than nothingness?" and Camus' "Why not suicide?". In the present age, it seems that we are provided with many vehicles to help us eliminate the pain of being a subject, and the integrity of thought that supports the illusion of a coherent "I".

Perhaps being, relating and existing as a "first person" now feels too problematic. The postmodernist critique that the subject was an illusion probably constituted the first philosophical objectification of subjective suicide. But now it seems that the shift away from the generation of meaning has destroyed selves in a different way: it has left them without agency, existing as objects in the world of objects.

Notes

1 Don DeLillo. *Cosmopolis*. New York, Scribner, 2003.
2 Simon Head. *Mindless: Why Smarter Machines Are Making Dumber Humans*. New York, Basic Books, 2014.
3 A neologism intended to signify the fusion of speed, the internet and social networking.
4 "Action thought" is an important idea of Heinz Kohut's which bears on my use of the term operationalism. See Heinz Kohut. *The Restoration of the Self*. New York, International Universities Press, 1977, pp. 36–48. Also see "the organizing personality" in

Lawrence Hedges. *Listening Perspectives in Psychotherapy*. Northvale, NJ, Jason Aronson, 1983, pp. 225–64.

5 The clinical samples in this book are derived from Anglo-American analysands. Psychoanalysts from other cultures may, therefore, be somewhat puzzled by these examples and if so may wish to substitute new forms of expression emerging in their own cultures.

6 For an interesting discussion of the limit of horizontal thinking see George S. Klein. *Perception, Motives, and Personality*. New York, Alfred Knopf, 1970, pp. 130–31.

7 There is a considerable literature on the concept of "the spectacle" beginning with the work of Guy Debord and the "situationists" of the mid-twentieth century.

8 Of course, the analysand's quizzical response is not a resistance but an unconscious request for further analysis. So, although he is refractive, horizontalizing and operationalizing, he is also unconsciously receptive to the analyst's comment.

9 Jameson's critique of contemporary culture in *Postmodernism: Or the Cultural Logic of Late Capitalism*. Durham, NC, Duke University Press, 1991 is the benchmark for all such studies of the late twentieth century. While I disagree with much of his argument – and with his idiosyncratic formulations of psychoanalytical theory – his work is brilliant and intellectually inspiring. There are many works that comment on the death of the subject, but a crucial late twentieth-century text is Alain Badiou. *Theory of the Subject*. London, Continuum, 2009 [1982]. Probably the foremost psychoanalytical cultural critique of the twenty-first century is Slavoj Žižek. *Living in the End Times*. London, Verso, 2010.

10 See John Steiner. *Psychic Retreats*. London, Routledge, 1993.

9

Resuscitation

In the last chapter we considered how certain forms of thinking, increasingly evident in the twenty-first century, may be driven by the demands of the globalized world for the more efficient self. We shall now review the changes that have taken place in the ego, and discuss how – at the individual level – those changes could be addressed in the therapy room, viewed here as a model for how we might think in more creative ways.

When people who have been physically tortured are freed from their captors, the way they walk and try to speak shows that their way of being has been compromised. Those who are otherwise oppressed over long periods of time may also show changes in the way they think, talk and relate, and I have described a constellation of mental forms that I propose are evidence of cumulative oppression.

Horizontalism eradicates hierarchical thinking, rendering mental contents equal. No one idea has more merit than another.

Homogenization eliminates difference and fuses diversity into the agglomerated. Efforts to distinguish ideas from one another are defeated.

Operationalism is a type of "action-thought" (to quote Kohut[1]) in which reflectiveness is immediately converted into a plan of action.

Refraction also replaces reflection, by shattering the integrity of an idea and dissolving its fragments into a stream of thoughts stripped of meaning.

Sight replaces insight. Visual experiences are sought as truths-in-themselves in a world that displaces language with images. The production, transmission and consumption of images are all accomplished with remarkable speed: a form of thinking I am terming sightophilia.

Unlike instincts, affects or memories, these patterns of thought are not endogenous formations responsive to intrapsychic forces; they are mentalities promoted by contemporary culture to which the ego will create adaptations. They therefore lack the complex interlacing imbrication of a self's profoundly idiosyncratic psychodynamic. However, although they are developed primarily within social psychology rather than being driven from the depths of individual psychic life, they may eventually become permanent structures in our mind. The price of civilization now is that selves are dominated less by a superego than by an ego that diminishes internal capabilities through deeply compromised forms of thinking.

The return of the repressed – a necessary focus for early twentieth-century psychoanalysis – refers to the reappearance of unwanted mental *contents* through disguised articulation. We are now considering a related idea, which I am calling *the return of the oppressed*. This refers, not to mental contents, but to new *forms* of thinking that are the result of oppression: reflective thought replaced by refractive shimmering; linguistic articulation transformed into cryptic sound bites; historical understanding displaced by expedient confabulation.

Here the return of unwanted ideas is dealt with by rewording; the idea is presented as permissible (at least as far as consciousness is concerned), by means of disguised articulation. Unwanted forms of perception, thinking and communicating arrive as degraded structures of thought.

Both types of return involve alteration of the banished.

Both involve complex defences against mental pain.

Both aim to satisfy human wishes

The oppressed self must find compromised forms of expression, so that oppression emerges as a new form of being. The drive to return the repressed to consciousness can lead to intriguing symptoms, dreams, linguistic formulations and even artistic creations, but a self who is suffering from profound oppression will reveal impoverishments of thinking and affect. This can be understood as a form of mental suicide, or subjecticide, which offers the self an ego position in the new social order through the elimination of sophisticated forms of perception and thoughtfulness.

The five adaptive forms described above lead to a more efficient self. Each style of thinking reduces mental complexity and prepares a self for more successful integration into a world moving too quickly and heartlessly to spare time for the depths of our internal worlds.

Part of the challenge facing the present-day psychologist is how to restore interest in being a subject. What tools can the clinician use to analyse oppression and the return of the oppressed?

Some of the distorted thought-forms of the twenty-first century can manifest in vague or abstract speech that forecloses free association: "I suppose I had a kind of okay time last weekend"; "I had a row with my partner last night so I'm a bit bummed out today"; "Well . . . I didn't have a very good time at the conference, just sort of drifted off, you know . . ."

In these samples we see a $-K^2$ abstraction ($-K$ is subtractive thinking, aimed at undoing the knowable) that rids the self of contact with psychic reality through the expression of empty forms of thinking. Before the psychologist can start to make sense of what is being communicated in these summaries, s/he needs to know *in detail* about the experiences from which they are abstracted. To do this s/he must mentally resuscitate the analysand, and it can be helpful to turn to the quotidian to see if the patient can use lived experience to animate thought: "You did not have a good time at the conference?"; an inflected interrogative usually elicits elaboration.

As the defensive obfuscation of abstraction is lifted and details are provided, the person begins, unknowingly, to free associate. S/he may think s/he is simply recollecting the events of the day, but as s/he speaks s/he produces chains of ideas that are governed by an unconscious logic; his or her manifest ideas appear in a sequence that reveals latent thoughts. To quote Virginia Woolf, s/he enters the "poetry of existence".[3]

In time, these chains of ideas become the evidence produced by psychoanalysis, and both therapist and patient develop a "third ear" with which to listen to them. Free association creates new idioms of listening, intensifying and disseminating the self's ability to unconsciously comprehend the world. Although this has always been the case, in today's era of compromised thought processes, its significance becomes even more crucial.

As the patient speaks the details and the therapist gathers the patterns of thought, a vital intrasubjective object relation between conscious self and unconscious being becomes established. An intersubjective dynamic therefore fosters its intrasubjective twin; it evolves slowly, developing what we might think of as *dynamic consciousness* – consciousness that appreciates, receives and employs unconscious thinking with creative skill.

The psychic value of this realization is profound, and its conceptualization is the self's comprehension of what it is to be a subject: to be there as a conscious being, continuously and endlessly moved by one's idiomatic unconscious interests. In a psychoanalysis we speak in order to hear from the self.

The late twentieth century has been characterized as witness to the death of language ("linguisticide"), giving way to sign-systems of shared emotiveness, platitudes, clichés, and so forth. In this era of anodyne speech, to re-find more sophisticated uses of language is to empower the self as it turns towards the tasks of introspection. To discover, or rediscover, the *pleasure* of language constitutes an important emotional experience; verbal articulation releases suffocated affects and emotions that have been buried, foreclosed and compromised by degraded forms of thinking and a loss of interest in speech itself.

To describe the details of one's thoughts to an analyst is to establish, over months and then years, psychological day residue: daily reports and associations that provide access to moments of what Freud termed "high psychic value". This activity in itself generates dreams because the analytic relationship – I have called this the *Freudian pair*[4] – is there to receive them. Free association elicits curiosity. Where before there may have been little interest in the individual search for meaning, now the self is producing highly significant articulations, both conscious and unconscious, contributing to what Freud termed "the storehouse of ideas".

These days, however, we are seeing a rather intriguing reversal of the twentieth-century use of free association. Then, selves, meandering in the everyday, encountered objects in lived experience that gathered psychic momentum, creating experiences that demanded to be dreamed – nodal junctions for the dissemination of the meanings of that day. Now it seems that the retreat into the mentally denuded realms of the normopathic universe insulates the self against significance in the lived. People still dream, but analytical efforts to link the dream to the vivid events of the preceding day often fail. These moments of psychic intensity have not been registered by a self that, because it is defended against receiving them, is unable to form them into vertices of meaning.

In the twenty-first century, it seems that psychically significant day residue rarely appears spontaneously, but must be reconstructed from accounts of events in the real. It is the emotional experiences and epiphanies generated by free associations in the session that then produce a dream. So, whereas Freud conceptualized dreams as reflections on the psychic intensities of the *previous* day, they seem now to transfer mental significance forwards, into the lived experiences of the *following* day, animating the object world with a vitality and meaning that has been missing. The dream, then, emerges as an inspiration to the self; as an act of creativity vital to sustaining the human imagination.

Notes

1   See Heinz Kohut. *The Analysis of the Self*. New York, International Universities Press, 1971, p. 158. A more extended view of this form of thinking is to be found in his later book, *The Restoration of the Self*. New York, International Universities Press, 1977, pp. 36–48.

2   In Wilfred Bion's theory of thinking, K stands for knowledge and −K stands for statements that detract from knowing. A −K statement subtracts from the self's store of knowledge.
3   See Virginia Woolf. *A Writer's Diary*. New York, Harcourt Brace Jovanovich, 1982 [1953], p. 55.
4   The "Freudian pair" refers to the partnership of the analysand invested with free associating (or free talking) and the psycho-analyst who is in a meditative state (Freud termed it "evenly suspended attentiveness") in which he is "free listening". For a lucid description of the concept of the Freudian pair see Sarah Nettleton. *The Metapsychology of Christopher Bollas: An Introduction*. London, Routledge, 2016, pp. 74–82.

10

Anti-globalization

Civilizations have always been composed of groups co-existing in space and time but living in parallel worlds. The monastic realms of the religiously devout, the cluttered rooms of scientists whose work is incomprehensible to all but those of like kind, the intense and sequestered world of foreign-policy mandarins: there have been many different ways of living alongside one another in what we still term a society.

One of the outcomes of globalization is the creation of a new kind of "government". This parallel world is ruled to a considerable extent by individuals of wealth, power and influence, who operate empires derived from the increasing use of high-end technology. These demand the employment, and proximity, of a new class of workers – specialists in IT and AI. They maintain the engines that drive the offices and communication systems used by this new oligarchy, and they are also vested with the responsibility of inventing new forms of technology, with the aim of outstripping the competitors by creating further new forms of social organization.

Although the new oligarchs are not all of a kind – Warren Buffett and Bill Gates are well-intentioned philanthropists who are champions of democracy whilst a good many of Putin's oligarchs are not – the wealthy govern our lives in ways beyond our perception. At their disposal are populations of employees: their IT and AI staff are joined by economic forecasters and investment firms to guide their financial dealings, banks to handle the funds, research and development teams to develop their empires, whilst others further swell the coffers through marketing and public relations.

These new oligarchies are at home with globalization and, as they share many of the structural features involved, they are not paralysed by the complexity of the modern world. On the contrary, they are driving it, inventing and developing new ways of organizing our society, and in the process they are establishing positions of immense power. The complexity of modern globalized living has gone beyond the capacity of most people to comprehend it, and in 2016, with Brexit and the election of Trump, we see clear signs of backlash.

If we look back to previous times we can certainly find technological changes that shocked people – from trains in the early nineteenth century, to the telephone, then to air travel and the television in the twentieth century. Offensive to a sense of the "natural" order of things, perhaps, but these revolutions in travel and communication were not imposed as mandatory aspects of living. People could choose not to travel by train, use phones or planes, or watch TV and they could still be part of society.

So it is not the shock of change (Toffler's "future shock"[1]) in itself that is traumatizing; it is the overwhelming complexity of "dark matter". Like the workings of quantum mechanics, which governs the circuitry within our computers, the dark matter in the universe cannot be seen, but, like gravity, it is the glue that holds everything together. And there is a form of dark matter that is now operating our world.

The invisibility of the dark matter of globalization poses serious challenges to many people who have not been able to identify with the app universe. In a world of complexity, in which we each play our small transmissive part, many people seem to be in retreat.

These retreats may take the form either of organized small group opposition to globalization, or of radical alternatives to it. We see this in "sustainable living" communities, a somewhat Luddite rejection of the new industrial revolution that is increasingly attractive to a wide range of often the educated and privileged, in the West. Some of the rejections of globalization go back into the mid-twentieth century, early indications that the increasing complexity of the world was proving, for some, to be too great a challenge.

If we look at the increase in the active effect of the world's religions, especially Christianity and Islam, we see people who are retreating into a more simplified view of life. What is commonly termed "fundamentalism" could as well be named "anti-complexity". People who were already feeling lost due to the abandonment by their societies' leaders of the God they had worshipped for millennia were then faced with the emergence of a substitute – the growing power of market forces, there to serve the elite. Selves in retreat from the bewilderment of the modern world wanted simpler rules for living, and some found relief in a fervent, shared obedience to a God who was there for the ordinary man and woman.

At first, the Obama presidency signified *inclusiveness*. Obama shared the anti-Washington rhetoric of Tea Party conservatives, running on a platform that portrayed the capital as corrupt and in need of profound change. In 2016, many of those in places such as Michigan and Wisconsin who had seen hope in Obama would vote for Trump – and a completely different political agenda – not because they were attending to the policy differences between the two, but because they wanted to vote against Washington, DC. Although some within the Trump base were certainly hard-right zealots, many others were not. To blame the government was to protest about being governed by forces outside their perception, and certainly outside their control.

After two terms of Obama, eight years after the crash of 2008, the public had seen no prosecutions of the bankers on Wall Street; instead they had witnessed an intensification of globalization, associated with big money and capitalist expansionism at the expense of the American middle class. They were shown a handsome, virile president with his beautiful wife and daughters hanging out with celebrity after celebrity at a White House that could have been Hollywood East. For however inspiring Obama was, and however enlightened many of his policies, by 2016 his social life – at least as it played out on the television screens of middle-class rural America – seemed elitist, privileged, self-idealizing and profoundly out of touch.

The political changes across the West in 2016–17 – Trump's victory, Brexit, the rise of Le Pen – were multinational and diverse. What forces could lead to shifts towards the right in so many parts of the world?

The populations of these very diverse countries were united by a frame of mind. People felt profoundly alienated by the world around them, and although the disaffected right wing were anti-immigrant and anti-government, many others were simply exhausted by the struggle to meet the rising cost of living with inadequate wages. There would be common agreement across the political spectra that a significant proportion of the populations were voting against globalization, and in favour of a return to nationalism. Attracted by what was, at times, a dangerously oversimplified view of the world, they were protesting against complexity.

By turning to a vision of problems solved by building "a great big wall", or throwing out the Muslims, or promoting national isolation and military solutions to international problems, society could be redefined and understood. The turn towards creationism and away from evolution theory is as much a turning away from the complexity (and remoteness) of the sciences as it is a resurgence of belief in a theory of our origins. By rejecting the sciences, millions could turn away, too from the alarming spectre of climate change and the confusion of energy policies that meant doing away with familiar sources of power. So many facets of the world seemed to be disappearing right before their eyes. The idea of a move away from complexity towards a new simplicity brought relief, and this was consolidated as they found themselves part of interlocking communities of like-minded people all over the world. But the refusal to accept the complexity, of life and of the mind, does not come without a price.

The qualities in Trump that were so offensive to the East and West Coast elites – his florid displays of sexism, racism, vulgarity, violence and vengefulness – were intended to convey that he was, unlike all the politically correct "fakes", just one heck of an honest human being. By celebrating the bad sides of being a self, in a kind of revivalist attempt to include all sinners, Trump inverted Christianity into a celebration of our worst characteristics. This came in the form of a "new honesty": "We owe it to each other and to our God, to fess up and just speak it like it is. Let God judge us, but whatever else we do, let's be true to who we really are down within our hearts."

His supporters were no doubt unaware that he was usurping real fears and frustrations with a form of pleasure, but in the viscera of affect they found feeling-based responses in a form of mental ecstasy that lifted them out of chronic disenchantment. It was fun to hate the Obamas, gay marriage, environmentalists, the transgender, or just about anyone who wasn't from where they were from. It meant that the world could be divided along ancient Christian lines: between good and evil, between the armies of Christ and those of Lucifer.

And as people congregated in their churches, cafes and bars, at their community dinners, fairs, harvests and round-ups, they could see that they were amongst decent, God-fearing people – "good" people. Their beliefs must be the right ones because you could trust what you could see. How could you possibly have faith in a world that you could not judge with your own eyes? You might tune into Rush or Hannity on local radio to get an affect boost of outrage that united you with kindred spirits all over the country, but otherwise why would you ever be stupid enough to believe what you read in the *New York Times* or saw on CNN? Newspapers and cable news simply circulated the same old lies promoted by the powers-that-be – the "liberal elite". The media was part of the problem. Not to be trusted. In a state of *collective hate*, millions of people found that the pleasures of emotional evacuation brought something approaching peace of mind.

Hate and peace of mind?

In the age of bewilderment, there was peace to be found in ridding the mind of unwanted complexity. This was another "born-again" experience, as believers were purified of invasive contaminants that threatened the self's spiritual way of life. Emotions, not "facts" (the stuff that made selves miserable), would be the new criteria of receptive intellection.

If thinking something made you feel better, it had to be right; if ideas made you feel worse, then they were bad and to be eliminated.

The act of mental evacuation is not indiscriminate; it requires specific "objects" that will receive the eliminated, rather like toilets that are designed for targeted eliminations. One might be designated for the corrupting pronouncements of science; another for the oppressive regulations of the federal government. The elimination of regulatory requirements could even bring the bliss of lawlessness.

The anti-globalization movement, which certainly houses legitimate critiques, has been co-opted in support of a xenophobic retreat into regional, ethnic, religious or political enclaves. This movement corresponds to what Freud meant by the "death drive": a self's retreat from a non-familiar world into the enclave of the secluded self. Juxtaposed to this is the life drive, in which selves invest in multiple and diverse objects that enable them to expand their interests and radiate their potential in creative ways.

Globalization may be replete with hazards, and investment in worlds far beyond one's own has sponsored both colonialism and capitalism. In some ways it is less dangerous to the self than the death drive, but, as we shall see, the globalized world creates further complex dilemmas.

Note

1   See Alvin Toffler. *Future Shock*. New York, Bantam, 1990 [1970].

11

The democratic mind

We associate the birth of democracy, in Athens in the fifth century BCE, with the beginning of democratic politics. The democratic process has in fact been traced by some back to much earlier hunter-gatherer communities, but when Solon led the establishing of democracy in Greece, he instantiated important new political structures: the right of all free male citizens to vote, the right to hold office, selection by lots and not by favour. There was also the right to express one's view in the assembly, and this reflected the wisdom of including as many points of view as possible in the governing process.

The downsides of this system were obvious. As discussed earlier, by refusing the right of women and slaves to be part of the democracy, the Athenian polis was deprived of the vitality of crucial differences of gender and race – prejudices that became instantiated as part of the democratic process in the West.

Democracy was complex and time consuming – during times of war, the democratic process would be compromised or even suspended – and it required the group had to bear up under the stress of conflicting views that might be driven by questionable if not nefarious aims. But the alternatives – tyranny, oligarchy, monarchy – were considered to be worse. So democracy had in its favour both what it was and what it was not.

The right of each free male to speak his mind meant that, for some, profoundly opposing positions were allowed the space of representation. In so many ways, this axiom – speak what you think, your thoughts will be displaced by the next speaker – has parallels with the experience of the speaking self in a psychoanalysis. For in the analytical space, although the "I" presumes to preside over all of the self's views, in fact this is a nominal position. The thoughts that cross a mind are diverse and contradictory, with some too heinous to be borne by consciousness. The process is founded on the analyst's pledge of neutrality. He or she will not intervene in such a way as to prevent any ideas from being expressed; on the contrary, the self's minority views, which could so easily be silenced, are urged into articulation. The analytical relationship creates a psychological democracy.

There will be moments when the analysand may find this freedom embarrassing, or shocking, or surprising, but in time it allows consciousness to discover the complex views held by any self, within what analysts term "the internal world". This universe of thought and feeling, which we all have in common, is ordinarily kept a deep, dark secret in the world of human intersubjectivity, but in a psychoanalysis, and within a democracy, the self, or the group, is encouraged to speak without censorship. The citizen of Athens also had the right to be represented. Those who were not elected to attend the assembly and take part directly could still expect to have their views expressed and heard.

For hundreds of years, and especially from the eighteenth century onwards, politicians in Europe would debate the pros and cons of democracy and how it could be institutionalized, in full or in part. In doing this, unknowingly perhaps, Europeans were constructing a theory of both the individual and the group mind as a *representative agency*. A philosophy of government was following and realizing a psychic need.

John Stuart Mill[1] was a crucial figure in this evolution, and he thought of "the modern mind" (44) as owing a great deal to "the powerful dialectics" of Socrates" (44). Mill's vision of liberty (in effect, the democratic process) was dependent upon what he termed "reflecting persons" (8). He wondered why people were capable of "rational opinions and rational conduct" and he concluded that this must be "owing to a quality of the human mind" in which the reflective self seeks the company of others who will subject his own views to opposing ones.

He is capable of rectifying his mistakes by discussion
and experience. Not by experience alone. There must be
discussion, to show how experience is to be interpreted.
Wrong opinions and practices gradually yield to fact and
argument: but facts and arguments, to produce any
effect on the mind, must be brought before it.

(22)

We see here a preview of the psychoanalytical axiom that
the reflecting self benefits from *talking* and engaging the
other in discussion. Mill continues:

Because he has kept his mind open to criticism of his
opinions and conduct. Because it has been his practice to
listen to all that could be said against him; to profit by as
much of it as was just, and expound to himself, and upon
occasion to others . . . because he felt that the only way
in which a human being can make some approach to
knowing the whole of a subject, is by hearing what can
be said about it by persons of every variety of opinion,
and studying all modes in which it can be looked at by
every character of mind.

(22)

Discussing the duties of the listening orator (referring
to Cicero), he states, "the rational position for him would be
suspension of judgement". He must "feel the whole force of
the difficulty which the true view of the subject has to
encounter and dispose of; else he will never really possess
himself of the portion of the truth which meets and removes
that difficulty" (37). Mill understood that the listening self
had to endure the full weight of the other's points of view, not
simply as cognate phenomena – intellectual objects – but as
powerful emotional experiences. This statement could easily
be the credo of the psychoanalyst who, from his position of
neutrality, must subject himself to the full force of the analysand's emotional life if he is to understand the unconscious
truths embedded in his statements.
    Although Mill's listening position is remarkably like
that of the psychoanalyst, his interventions tend to be more

rhetorical: "there are good reasons for remonstrating with him, or reasoning with him, or persuading him, or entreating him" (13). He acknowledges the problems posed by "pre-judices or superstitions; often social affections, not seldom their antisocial ones, their envy or jealousy, their arrogance or contemptuousness". However, he argues that such feelings are part of the universal need to act in "self-interest" (10). This doctrine of self-interest is what today we would term a narcissistic defence: the person projects his own opinions onto others and assumes them to be universal. Any other views are simply wayward or incorrect. Mill writes: "The practical principle which guides them to their opinions on the regulation of human conduct, is the feeling in each person's mind that everybody should be required to act as he" (9).

Mill was born in 1806 and died in 1873; his life there-fore spanned most of the nineteenth century. His essays on the reflecting self were a considerable step forward in the understanding of how a democracy works.

It is surely no accident that the most important modern work on democracy – "On Liberty" – derived in large part from conversations Mill had with his wife Harriet Taylor Mill, just one year before her death. The work embodies his wife's views, providing the vital presence of the female other that allow the mind to expand and deepen the listening process, so salient to the Mill's view of democracy. Mill would then proceed in 1869 to write *The Subjection of Women*, which included his wife's views, which were clearly deeply influential, as well as the comments of his daughter, Helen Taylor, with whom he also collaborated on the work. The Mill family's vision, then – at last bringing women into the writings on democracy – demonstrated his theory in a profound and moving manner, some two thousand years after democracy had originally been established as the province of free male citizens.

The psychoanalyst Wilfred Bion was born in 1897 and died in 1979 and, like Mill, he may be seen as representa-tive of his century. However, as a tank driver during the Great War, Bion had witnessed the savagery of a conflict that challenged Mill's view of the possibility of a democracy that did not take into account the depth of human destructiveness. After World War One he trained in psychiatry and psychoanalysis, and he revolutionized psychoanalytical theory and practice through his work with groups, described in a series of publications, notably *Experiences in Groups* (1961).

The characteristics valued by Mill – the need of participants in a democracy to speak freely, the value to any reflecting self of undergoing powerful emotions stirred up by the views of others – were certainly shared by Bion. However, in his experiments in "social psychology", when he found himself inside the group mind, he arrived at a troubling discovery: if the psychoanalyst leaves the group members to themselves and declines to provide direction, they will slowly descend into primitive and, at times, highly disturbed states. In other words, minds are easily shut down by psychotic anxieties or primitive needs.

Mill, and others, had observed how democracy reflected the minds of those who took part, and they suggested that it required flexible and thoughtful selves. This was an important step towards the concept of democracy both as a theory of mind and as an observation on mental life itself. In my view, Bion's work and that of other group psychoanalysts in London *realized* the preconception that democracy was a recognition of how the mind worked. Without stating explicitly that a group was a democracy, or that it represented the democratic process, this is exactly what these analysts were exploring in the latter half of the twentieth century.

Bion's French biographer, Gérard Bleandonu[2] (himself a group psychoanalyst), wrote of Bion's concept of "leaderless groups": "in effect, it introduced a democratic principle into the process of selection by focusing on communal relational aptitudes" (57). The principle was illustrated by Bion's conviction that the selection of officers should depend on how the individual behaves within a leaderless group, thus opening up potential qualification to anyone.

In *Democracy and Dictatorship: Their Psychology and Patterns of Life,*[3] the Romanian social psychologist Zevedei Barbu followed an ancient tradition – one debated by Aristotle – that democracy required the right sort of citizen for it to be effective. In describing the characteristics of the "democratic state of mind", he suggested that it required "a specific *frame of mind*, that is, certain experiences, attitudes, prejudices and beliefs shared by them all, or by a large minority" (13).

In an important essay at the turn of the twenty-first century, Adam Phillips[4] explored ways in which Bion's groups – and any group process predicated on psychoanalytical assumptions – make us all into "equals", the title of his essay. He pursues many lines of thought, including the idea that differences between people will make some less equal than others, even if in principle we have the right to equality.

He suggests that psychoanalysis is a form of democracy – indeed "the aim of psychoanalysis ... might be the pre-condition for democracy" (17). Ultimately it will reveal the forms of authority embedded in any self, the "anti-democratic voices and urgings and their complex history" (24). This notion derives from Freud's censorship model of the unconscious. Even though one wants, and tries, to free associate, a part of the mind steps in to censor and distort what might otherwise have been said.

However, even though this censorship does exist, if the analysand keeps on talking, moving from one patch of discourse to another, then whether s/he knows it or not, s/he will always reveal patterns of unconscious thinking. But these chains of thought that reveal the narrative of the unconscious do not remain incontestable. A few minutes, days or weeks later, the self may reveal quite different views. Walt Whitman had a clear sense of the dialectic of the free association of people and ideas in his celebration "Song of Myself". He writes: "Do I contradict myself? / Very well then I contradict myself; (I am large, I contain multitudes.)" [5]

Above all else, free associations reveal how full of contradictions we are. Within a group, it is not so much that one person speaks for ideas that are anathema to others, although this may seem to be true at certain points. In fact, any person speaking for long enough will unconsciously disclose a wide range of views, some of which would offend their conscious mind. Given enough time (and that is one thing that the analytic approach does provide), as they "gossip" about life they will disclose many hidden aspects of the human mind, often unaware, in their light-hearted perambulations, that they are letting the cat out of the bag

I was trained in Bion groups at the Tavistock Clinic in the early 1970s. At that point the Tavistock had become the centre of a movement: scores of clinicians from around the world would train there in order to learn how to conduct a new form of group psychoanalysis. Unique to the "Tavi Group" was a particular interpretive approach: whatever any member of the group said at any time was to be understood as representative, in some way, of all members of that group. This axiom was realized through a simple rhetorical position.

A fictional (condensed) example:

Jim (breaking down in tears): "Bob, I have tried and tried to get you to understand me."

Bob: "You are just so thick and rejecting – I feel there's really no point in talking to you."

Analyst: "The group is not sure how to proceed. When one does not feel understood it is tempting to find someone to be responsible for that."

Jane: "I don't feel that what Jim has said is something I would ever have said to Bob."

Analyst: "The group is uncomfortable having to contain all the differing elements of the self, especially angry and distressed ones."

By interpreting in this way, the analyst facilitates the continued representation of the issues being expressed: "I don't feel understood", "people are too thick to bother with", "I can't align myself with aggressive behaviour". Because these thoughts are reworded as a *group position*, nobody is isolated for being in the wrong, or left to fight it out. Jim might feel irked at Bob's irritation, but the analyst's intervention indicates that his feeling of not being understood is an ordinary one, common to all members of the group. In this way, even seemingly extreme states of mind are transformed into bearable ideas that can then be thought about.

One of the functions of the group leader is to hold on to complex situations within the group rather than getting rid of them by smoothing them out. Bion referred to this as the function of the container in relation to the contained, and he maintained that the act of interpretation derived from the analyst's "reverie". This deceptively simple formulation opened up new vistas in technique, emphasizing a form of analytic listening that relied on an unconscious capacity in the analyst.

For my part, I found in Bion's methodology a remarkable realization of working democracy. The idea that any individual speaker was speaking for the entire group was a revelation. The theory did not assume, of course, that anything said in the room spoke for all other members of that group right there and right then; it meant that each member of the group would at certain moments experience those same sorts of feelings.

When the group analyst makes what we might think of as a democratic intervention – "the group thinks that . . ." – s/he slows the process down, reducing the likelihood of any individual acting upon the violence of impulse. Jim has launched an attack on Bob which in other circumstances might lead to a violent encounter, but when it is reworded as a thought that could be voiced by any member, the idea is immediately *democratized*. "We are all in this together."

What we learned, both as participants in Tavi Groups and then as leaders, was that a group included all the elements that make up *homo sapiens*: all the good things about us and all the bad things would emerge in that room, but no one was to be singled out. There were no saints and no sinners.

Bion's approach creates what D.W. Winnicott termed "a potential space". The group has the opportunity to express and consider any thoughts that arise out of the idea that has been expressed – in our example this might be the idea that we are vulnerable, or anger about feeling isolated and not understood. And as the members of the group pick up each of these lines of thought, they will become ramified into many diverse and divergent associative strands. Over time, these will grow into matrices of associations that this group will have assembled as a result of Jim's distress and Bob's defences against the complexity of group life.

Working in this way, one therefore discovers within the democratic process its therapeutic effect: democratization disseminates divergent emotions or ideas through many people who will elaborate, contextualize and render them differently. The eventual accomplishment of understanding will be the work of the group, as it gradually forms its own mind according to psychic democracy, entertaining all the conflicting ideas and feelings experienced by its members.

As a process, I found this deeply liberating, and I found its principles applicable in many ways to work with individuals in psychoanalysis. For example, when discussing toxic parts of the personality, or disturbing ideas, I might say: "A part of you is furious with me and wants to wipe out what I have said, but I have also heard from other parts of you that are wrestling with those very powerful feelings."

I am sure I was also influenced in this by Paula Heimann, my first analytical supervisor, who would ask, in relation to a particular moment in a session: "Who is speaking, to whom, about what, and why now?" This showed me that any mind could simultaneously house many speakers, talking to various others about all kinds of things.

At times I might liken the mind to a democratic assembly, perhaps using the British Parliament or the American Congress as extended metaphors. I noticed that no one ever challenged this idea; indeed, it was as if we all knew it to be an appropriate analogy. This existential realization of the viability of the metaphor confirmed for me the idea that the concept of democracy was as applicable to our internal world as it was to conflicts amongst groups and nations.

In an earlier essay I argued that we all have a "representative drive":[6] an urge to express our views. This drive arrives out of the *jouissance* of the infant and toddler over expression and then speech. We might see this drive, so necessary to the self's expression of idiom, as the psychic foundation of the force behind democracy; something that arrives, not because it has been handed down over the centuries, but because it exists within all of us as an intrinsic feature of the need to speak freely.

This has a bearing on the debates over whether certain countries – in North Africa or the Middle East – could ever become democracies. In the Arab Spring, it was striking that people naturally formed groups in which the democratic principle was assumed, even though this had never been part of their political environment. But if we understand this principle as inherently psychologically familiar to us, then it should come as no surprise that even those with no experience of this type of government will choose to form a democratic process.

So when we think of what is required of democratic government, we are simultaneously conceptualizing, not simply a frame of mind, but mind itself. The different dimensions of democracy – as a mental feature of an open mind and as the political expression of government shared by all – reinforce one another. As Fukuyama[7] states: "Between 1970 and 2010, the number of democracies around the world increased from about 35 to nearly 120, or some 60 percent of the world's countries" (399). When he asks himself why this is so, he first cites the school of thought that believes "democracy has taken hold as the result of the power of the underlying idea of democracy" (400) and he links this tradition to Hegel, and the view that "the working out of the inner logic of human rationality" (400) naturally leads to the democratic frame of mind.

In my view, the idea that democracy follows from the logic of human reason is incorrect. Indeed, the reasoned self evolves gradually out of an *internal* democracy of many competing ideas that, in the beginning, might more accurately be described as mental chaos.

Eventually – and by "the Age of Reason" – people became more familiar with the idea of the mind's sometimes incoherent cacophony, and, though from a somewhat distanced inner perspective, they began to trace the hidden logical features of what had seemed nonsensical. What Freud maintained was that there exist within the chaos of the unconscious "clusters of thought" ideas that, when grouped together, form the basis of coherent views. In time, these unconscious clusters of meaning act as internal force fields (the ancient Greeks saw the mind as an arena through which forces passed, like the wind) that may be objectified, or made conscious. The technique of "free association" showed that a seemingly incoherent sequence of discontinuous ideas would reveal "latent contents" that were governed by an underlying logic of their own. This ramifying network of unconscious thinking required dynamic consciousness in order to be spoken, communicated and understood.

Although, as Freud's theory showed, the unconscious self is inherently democratic, this state of mind may easily be compromised by powerful feelings that evoke other forms of self or group governance. These include the totalitarian position, the moment when a self makes a decision based upon great force emanating from within the personality, or the oligarchic situation, in which a group of people forms a governing mentality, or the monarchial state, when an individual adopts a princely view of the world.

Just as we all know of our internal democratic process, we also know of our totalitarian, oligarchic and monarchical tendencies. They are part of who we are. These frames of mind do not arrive from the outside world, in handed-down texts or ancient laws of governance; they are predicated on structures that exist within our internal world. And they are mental and psychological pathways we may take at any time. Whereas the democratic frame of mind will happily house many diverse ideas – "democratic vistas", to quote Walt Whitman – the totalitarian frame of mind will shut down the divergent voices of our inner democracy to follow a narrow, rigid set of views.

Like the Greeks, any group that uses the democratic process will discover that this is hardly a frame of mind suited to quick thinking or immediate action. Those who constructed the US Constitution understood this, when, in forming the American democracy, they created a system of checks and balances. It was a laborious process, and they intended it to be this way. They knew that in a country already as diverse and complex as the original Thirteen Colonies, people would need to represent many conflicting issues of economics, ethnicity and class. They had to form a government that would neither descend into mob rule (a fear prominent in the eighteenth-century mind, given the events of the French Revolution) nor revert to a monarchial system.

The American electorate would continue to be highly diverse, even though some values would be shared in common, but some time in the early twenty-first century, there was a growing impatience across both party lines and throughout the United States with what was to become known as "the do nothing Congress". Before the dawn of this century, Senators and Members of the House would "cross the aisle" and form alliances between differing representatives so that many positions or views could join one another under compromise. The various parties of the Congress strove to understand why other representatives took the positions they did, and with that understanding, as democratically elected citizens, they created laws.

However, after 9/11 and the War in Iraq, and in the face of the remarkable pace of globalization and climate change (yes, strange cousins these), the sheer complexity of the world bore down upon the citizens of the Western world, especially in the United States. First al-Qaeda and then ISIS (Daesh) successfully terrorized the West, which quickly lost sight of why these people had taken up arms in the first place. As panic set in, patience with the democratic way of thinking gave way to a fear that America was not properly protecting itself.

The reasons for the arrival of Daesh were complex and understandable, but Americans disconnected Daesh's raison d'être from their terrorist actions. Many were probably aware that these people were not simply Muslims; they were Sunni Arabs, displaced by the invasion of Iraq and angry at the Shias' failure to protect them following the invasion. However, by this time America was fed up with the conflicts in the Middle East, and they renounced these more complex factors. More to the point, they began to renounce the complexities of thought in general. From a group relations perspective, the subtle dimensions of the picture were no longer being represented in Congress or in the minds of the American citizens, and the fragility of both forms of democracy – of state and of mind – was to manifest itself in the startling fact that a country that had elected the African American Obama in 2008 and 2012 could choose Trump in 2016.

The metaphor of the mind as a democracy, with different points of view and with numerous representatives and styles of representing, points, perhaps, to an unconscious dimension in the intentions of the Athenians. The founding of democracy depended on a process of psychological change that began from within, but the Greeks were able to introduce an organizing structure that institutionalized these changes so that the social sculptures of the polis provided freedom for mental representation.

As discussed, the technological revolutions of the twenty-first century have threatened our capacity to maintain traditional forms of meaning within the fabric of the new industrial world. Democracies have become infiltrated and undermined by powerful but shadowy corporations, many of a totalitarian bent, and political parties and elected representatives have opted for the politics of polarization rather than the democratic tasks of inclusiveness, discussion and compromise. It would be hardly surprising if selves were no longer so inclined to exercise a democratic frame of mind.

The evolution of democracy, over thousands of years, is amongst our greatest accomplishments. Although it may come and go according to the emotional state of a person or a nation, the democratic process remains a *potential* in all human beings, even within the most totalitarian self. If we appear to be losing our collective and individual capacity to sustain a democratic frame of mind, we may take solace in knowing that, given the right group conditions, it can return.

In the next chapters we shall turn to those forces that threaten our internal democracy.

Notes

1   See John Stuart Mill. "On Liberty" in *John Stuart Mill: On Liberty, Utilitarianism, and Other Essays*. Oxford, Oxford University Press, 2015 [1859], pp. 5–112.

2   See Gérard Bleandonu. *Wilfred Bion: His Life and Works 1897–1979*. London, Free Association Books, 1994.

92   THE DEMOCRATIC MIND

3   See Zevedei Barbu. *Democracy and Dictatorship: Their Psychology and Patterns of Life*. London, Forgotten Books, 2015.
4   See Adam Phillips. *Equals*. New York, Basic Books, 2002.
5   See Walt Whitman, "Song of Myself" in *Walt Whitman The Complete Poems*. London, Penguin, 2004, p. 123.
6   See Christopher Bollas. *The Evocative Object World*. London, Routledge, 2010.
7   See Francis Fukuyama. *Political Order and Political Decay: From the Industrial Revolution to the Globalization of Democracy*. New York, Farrar, Straus & Giroux, 2014.

12

"I hear that . . ."

The Friends and Neighbors Café is the hub of the small North Dakota village of Tolna (population 157). Some 1780 miles from California, it is a long way from the Rose Café in more ways than one.

It opens around 6 in the morning – earlier if they have customers dropping by for a bit of coffee – and by 7 a.m. it is buzzing. Farmers and locals meet up there, much as they did half a century ago when they were in grade school or high school. Only now they have families to attend to, as well as crops, farm machinery and town maintenance. They must meet the seasonal challenges if they are to survive.

In the mid-1990s I found a farmstead some fifteen miles south of the village. It took nearly fifteen years for most folks to know how to address my family, and longer for them to start to talk to us. We were the first "outsiders" in Nelson County; the locals had known one another since childhood, as had their parents and grandparents, going back to the late nineteenth century. It was common for people in their sixties to have great-grandchildren.

When I am staying alone on the farmstead I tend to go into town for breakfast around 6 a.m., and I sit in my usual place. (Folks tend to eat at their regular tables, rather like Europeans bagging sun loungers on the shores of Greek islands.) The waitresses are reserved but kind, and every few weeks they will ask how things are going out on my farm: Have I seen the pack of coyotes? Are the deer still in my woods? Do I need someone to cut my hedge? The men discuss who has bought a new combine harvester, what the news is on commodities or how the crops are going, and share stories of hunting or fishing.

For twenty years I never heard anyone talk politics in Tolna as there is nothing visibly American about the place. (I often tell visiting Europeans that this might as well be Uzbekistan.) Main Street is bleak and empty, as if the town has had open heart surgery so that the huge farm machines can pass through its centre, advertising the serious intent of this distant outpost.

At day's end – except when planting or harvesting – the locals decant at L&J's Bar, next door to Friends and Neighbors. Thursday is "steak night" and the place is packed. Some days I'll get there around 5 p.m. and stay for an hour or so. When I arrive, most people are at the bar, fifteen butts on stools, backs to the door, everyone looking straight ahead in silence, nursing a beer for forty minutes or so. It is rather reminiscent of a meeting of the Society of Friends. Every so often someone will say something out of nowhere, and to nobody in particular. Often enough no one replies, unless Julie or Leyland is there, in which case the speaker might be rewarded with something like, "Well . . . you can sure say that again."

In around 2012, L&J's updated the bar by mounting two TV sets on the wall. People would then sit looking at the screens. It would be sitcoms or quiz shows – *Wheel of Fortune* was a favourite – and on Sundays in the season there would be the Vikings game. The local news would go on when the weather was problematic, which it often was in Dakota; otherwise no one watched the news proper.

But suddenly, in 2015, people were captivated by the Republican primary. I remember asking Julie what she thought of Trump – I think it was the first political question I had popped in twenty years. Julie laughed and said she didn't know; we agreed that he was so feckless that he was entertaining, and the conversation returned to more serious matters, such as whether Orville had managed to get fresh eggs for us all that day, or whether Stump Lake was doing okay after two weeks of non-stop lightning storms.

Rural North Dakotans do not have time to read the newspapers, or if they do have the time, they don't choose to.

They have precious little interest in state, national or international affairs. Instead, over breakfast at Friends and Neighbors they will pass local news around in 140 verbal characters:

Dan: "I hear Alec had a problem with the hedgerow."
   Silence.
Chuck: "It's them wires left near his barn."
   Silence.
Barry: "Them wires can be a problem."

This discourse is reliable; it is telegraphic, emotionally economical, news sanctioned by word of mouth.

And then, a break-out moment:

"I hear them guys are out there by Carol's place looking at the coulee."
   "Yup, they got plans with them."
   "I hear they dropped by an office in McVille yesterday."
   "Yeah . . . looking for some sort of paper to write stuff down on, I heard."

In the course of a few minutes this "breaking news" was passed around the tables, and by evening, when they met at L&J's, the whole town knew what was happening.

The "government" (federal, state and local) had planned for years to divert water from Spirit Lake south, running through the north side of Tolna, thus encroaching on their territory and sensibility: enough to rile farmers to near violent protest. These are people not generally inclined towards political action – at least not in this part of Dakota – but when they decided to put pitchforks and rifles in the back of their trucks and head out of town towards the east end of Stump Lake, they were "going to take on the government". They were ready for anything and my fear was that this could turn nasty.

The local paper reported that a small group of farmers had shown up to meet with government employees at the coulee;[1] the police only turned up to direct the traffic. In fact the police had been there to defuse a potentially violent encounter,[2] but perhaps the discrepancy between the two versions of reality was the result of a simple agreement to keep matters under control. Later, at L&J's, Julie was to say: "Well, you know, anything can happen."

When I first heard Trump cite his infamous source of news – "I don't know, but I hear that . . ." – I realized he was speaking the same language as my fellow Dakotans. The oral tradition of transmitting news, at F&N or L&J's or on the phone, was what the farm communities used and trusted. Fast-breaking *local* news had to be conveyed at Friends and Neighbours or L&J's or on the phone; and although Trump was from New York, they knew him more as a TV celebrity. *The Apprentice* was a lot of fun to watch, especially when he fired people. In a tedious and predictable world, Trump was a character, a fun guy who folks talked about, enlisting him in local oratory so that eventually he became one of their own.

To listen to Rush Limbaugh or Hannity on the radio is to receive orally delivered news – straight out of the rural tradition. I had always wondered why these guys were screaming on the radio, and then I realized one day that it was probably because they had to be heard over the noise of a farmer's tractor or a trucker's rig.

By 2016, Dakotans had Trump intensely on their mind, as if they had awakened from dormant political slumber. To these people who had never been politically involved, it seemed that Trump's ignorance of politics offered a perfect marriage. A long way from the manufacturing world of Ohio and Michigan, even further from the coal mines of West Virginia and Pennsylvania or the Southwest states struggling with swelling populations of drug cartels, the farmers of Dakota felt passionately about Trump's key political messages, even though these issues had almost no bearing on their lives. What he said did not matter; he was reassuring people by emphasizing his contempt for information that he claimed to regard as confabulation. Dakotans had no time to read but they loved to listen to one long yarn after another, and they admired Trump for putting one over on contestant after contestant in the run-up to his nomination.

Trump's ignorance and penchant for "alternative facts", especially those provided by right-wing radio shows and conspiracy theorists, fitted comfortably within the rich oral traditions of the American Midwest and of most of America, in fact, outside the East and West Coasts and urban areas. His strategists looked at the electoral map and drew the obvious conclusion: he could win this election.

Trump's America (something like 40 per cent of the population) follows another feature of the oral tradition as opposed to the print media: it is energized, not by reality-tested, evidence-based facts, but by emotions. When President Trump did a U-turn on Syria and decided after all to bomb Assad's air field, he did so because he had been emotionally moved by what he had seen on television: young children and babies – "innocent babies, babies, little babies"[3] – who had been gassed. This was to be a "feeling-based" presidency. Trump was not one who would sit back in the rarefied, cold-blooded space of privilege, pronouncing on world affairs; he was the guy next door, the person who would go with you to the coulee pitchfork in hand. He was your war buddy.

The oral tradition segues easily into Twitter, which uses the written word but follows the "I hear that . . ." logic. It brings people together, denying difference and separation, forming a tight-knit sense of community around selected issues. Whether it is Mexicans raping our young girls, or abortionists killing our babies to be, or corrupt politicians sending American jobs to China or Mexico, the community sharing the matrix of those feelings draws ever closer together. Emotion, not reason, is the glue binding this type of group process.

As with other demagogic situations in Europe and around the world, Trump's base is fundamentally undemocratic. It is certainly inclusive, in that it binds its members around powerful issues, but it can brook no opposition or debate; it can only hate its opponents.

This frame of mind is not, of course, exclusive to the right wing. It is be found in any movement that constructs itself around passionate, unreasoned convictions and imagined enemies. It is to this kind of group process, and its ramifications and implications, that we turn in the next chapter.

Notes

1   A coulee is a drainage ditch or culvert through which water passes.
2   Without irony, the *Bismarck Tribune* stated that the protesters were "deadly serious" during the protest. See "Tolna Coulee Project" by Lauren Donovan in the *Bismarck Tribune*, 17 May 2011.
3   See Luke Harding. "'It had a big impact on me'—story behind Trump's whirlwind missile response", *Guardian* (online), 7 April 2017. www.the guardian.com/world/2017/apr/07/how-pictures-of-syrian-dead-babies-made-trump-do-unthinkable.

13

Paranoia

All of us can be paranoid.

In the "heat of the moment" we may abandon the complexity of a situation and opt for a simplistic version of reality. This can offer us a more self-friendly version of things; it sometimes feels pleasurable to edge out the riff-raff of multiple meanings, like unwanted immigrants in the mind. And as we can all have feelings or thoughts crossing our minds that are dubious, or wrong, or just plain bonkers, we are accustomed to offloading certain ideas by projecting them into other people, rather than taking our time to calm down and subject such thoughts to reflection and self-correction.

Generally, however, when we solve a problem through paranoid projection we are aware of this, and if we have verbalized our thoughts we may go beyond a correction and apologize for our "over-statement" because we know that more was put into words than should have been. This is a formal recognition of projective processes.

However, if we are part of a group that is inclined to project its "shit" into others, then matters become more complicated and not so simple to reverse. The group projection easily escapes reflective processes. So when Bush and Blair declared that Saddam Hussein was hiding away weapons of mass destruction, they were speaking for a part of the UK–US administrations that had managed to get themselves to believe this. There were plenty of leaders, from all political parties and in many countries, urging them to slow down. But Blair and Bush continued relentlessly onwards, not because Saddam Hussein posed any serious threat, but because they had worked themselves and their colleagues into such a lather of fury that the urge to annihilate him overcame their better judgement. Their attack on Baghdad, famously described as "shock and awe", showed very clearly who really had the weapons of mass destruction.

Did Blair and Bush realize this? It is highly unlikely. These otherwise quite decent men were caught up in a power-driven frame of mind that emptied them of self-regulatory responsibility, and they gave in to the pleasures of paranoia: dumping their bad stuff into the other was just impossible to resist.

The leaders of the United States are constantly proclaiming its superior military capacities, as the most powerful country on the earth. Might makes right. Assuming themselves to be "the good guys", Americans seem quite unaware that this is the stance of a menacing bully, threatening the rest of the world with massive military intervention unless they kow-tow. It seems hard to believe that so many people in positions of responsibility – elected representatives, members of the foreign services, military leaders who knew the costs of war – did not stop to ponder whether they might be setting up Hussein as a toilet for the projection of American shit.

Perhaps the anaesthetics of self-idealization were enough to dull that insight. A violent innocence accompanies the sanctimoniousness of a nation that proclaims itself the standard bearer of human rights, spreading democracy around the world, and this works to cleanse the nation of any guilt that might accrue from its high-handed, at times horrific, treatment of millions of people around the globe.

Projective identification – depositing a part of oneself into another person or a thing – can be subtle, and it sometimes requires some translation.

Trump exclaims that he will "build a great big wall" to keep out the Mexicans. At a time when Americans are fearful of invaders – ISIS, immigrants from Syria and anyone trying to lure American jobs overseas – scapegoating simplifies a highly complex set of fears. "Mexicans" can therefore be translated as "any unwanted person". Trump ostensibly (and improbably) intends to create a physical object to keep out the unwanted. As discussed, perhaps the wall stands for Trump's refusal to entertain complex issues.

Ironically, for a man who has closed his mental borders to the migration of ideas that any president must entertain in order to lead a nation in a thoughtful way, Trump is curiously open about the contents of his own mind.

He rarely attempts to conceal his personality from the media – his mental processes are much more visible than those of his more sophisticated colleagues, such as Hillary Clinton or Barack Obama. This may be in part because he is so accustomed to dealing with the unwanted through projective identification. That is, when he discloses something about himself he quickly shoves it into another.

When he pledges to "Make America Great Again", we could translate this as "Make *myself* great again". When he describes Mexicans as "rapists and criminals" this might translate as "I will get rid of my sexist attacks on women and my shady business dealings by putting them into Mexicans." He accuses the press of issuing "fake news", whilst he fabricates the "truths" he wishes to espouse; projecting this part of himself into journalists. And so it goes: "Crooked Hillary", who will not disclose her shady email dealings, stands for Trump who will not disclose his taxes; the chant of "lock her up" is an unconscious reference to the members of his team who may face jail for violating the law.

Who knows what this man really thinks, or who he really is? In some ways, it does not matter. His "persona" – the figure whom he casts into our view and by which he must be judged – is engaged in an endless stream of projective identifications. Whenever he attacks any person or any group, the electorate should ask, "What part of his persona is he projecting and why?"

This type of paranoid functioning is typical of the psychology of the demagogue. For the Greeks, the term "demagogue" referred to a mob leader. These days it has come to mean a leader whose representations of issues is highly selective, and who appeals to the masses because he offers simple solutions to complex matters, gauging the feelings of the society and organizing them into a political rhetoric.

This captures paranoid aspects of the people's imagination, which gather force as the demagogue encourages them to connect with powerful emotions.

Paranoia successfully reverses the course of anxiety. Fearful of being found out as corrupt and duplicitous, as sexist and racist, the paranoid cure for Trump is to find surrogates into whom those traits can be projected, and then to prosecute them. And to win an election – for *President* of the United States: what better cover-up than that? This is a type of model of cure for all citizens who feel that their failures can be transferred into others, whether it be shady financial dealings, offensive sexual relations, endemic and inherited hatred of people of colour or different gender or sexual orientation. Trump's "art of the deal" with the electorate was a quid pro quo in which a vote for him as president was an exoneration of all the crimes any self had committed.

And is it really any surprise that Trump's most famous verbal act – "You're fired!" – may well foretell his own impeachment? The fate of projective identifications is captured to some extent in the phrase, "What goes around, comes around." And yet, knowing that, Trump seems impatient with the process itself, egging it on, pushing it faster than need be, as if the laws of psychology irritate a man who, otherwise, would prefer to have everything his own way.

What might the Trump dynamic have to do with Brexit?

The decision of the British people to leave the European Union was understandable from a psychological point of view. For decades, many had felt the EU had increasingly come to represent the entitlement of a political elite in Brussels, who dictated to member countries too many aspects of everyday life – even which foods they could and could not eat – and imposed a punitive "value added tax". Its "value" to the average middle-class person seemed at best barely visible, and at worst a scam. With waves of migrants finding their way from North Africa, the Middle East and elsewhere, it was easy enough for a political leader, such as Nigel Farage of UKIP, to blame migrants for taking jobs, destroying the sense of community and generally muddying up the traditional British quality of life.

Encouraged by this interpretation of events, Brexit psychology migrated into British minds, disturbing what had been a sense of relative well-being. Soon the paranoid process was in full bloom: now it was tasty to hate, wonderfully cleansing – good riddance to bad rubbish! A bewildering world could be reduced to black and white (or whites versus blacks and shades of brown). In other words, Brexit was a vote to leave by the part of the self that was small-minded, vengeful and hate based. By confusing migrants with terrorists, by suggesting that the EU programme of open borders stole British jobs, a failing Tory government and disenchanted people who were indeed struggling to make ends meet (as they had for decades) had found their scapegoat. People far removed from the shores of this gentle isle were to blame. Surely.

Paranoid thinking works in the short term because it binds people around powerful affects, and simplifies complex ideas into digestible ones that appear cohesive and are therefore assumed to be correct. Through projection, it purifies selves of unwanted parts, so that what was internally disturbing – capable of producing persecutory anxiety, guilt and depression – is dumped into some faecal-other who can then be flushed from sight or annihilated.

When, for example, America nominated Iran for its "enemy of the decade" award, it selected a relatively weak military power that came with vehement anti-American rhetoric. Visibly foreign – definitely not a lookalike nation – it was clearly engaged in geopolitical terror politics, the poor man's version of a military. By picking on Iran as its enemy, America chose a weaker twin as an object into which it could project its xenophobia, military-muscle mentality and subversive activities. It could then depart with a squeaky clean sense of purity – realizing the American Dream at the expense of others: an almost perfect recycling programme.

So America *needed* Iran. Without its enemy twin the paranoid process would not work, and the binding, blinding force of that psychology could not be activated. Indeed, this would expose Americans to the dangerous prospect of self-examination, in which their "might is right" domination of the world might be subjected to intellectual challenge from many sources, including some from within their own country. The constant search for new back-up enemies thus remains part of the military-industrial-psychological complex manned by hawks, in both the Republican and Democratic Parties, who scour the earth looking for baddies whom it is convenient to hate.

The paranoid move is a curiously adaptive mental action. It is a retreat from the complexity of the situation and the reality of external others, into an intensified intrasubjective relation. The self becomes absorbed by the relation of the "I" to the "me": the dialogic idiom of internal conversation. And the more the self feels isolated and alienated from others, the more this dispossession seems to confirm the logic of paranoid retreat.

Paranoia is a powerful passion. A sulking child, temporarily at odds with the parents, will retreat into a self-enclosed mood that visibly cuts the self off from the world. In these moments the child feels deeply assured of his righteousness, and he is soothed by an intrasubjective paranoid intimacy, a unique love relation between the self that speaks and the self that thinks. "Is anything wrong, honey?" the mother asks, to be met with a sultry and defiant "no".

By adolescence most of us stop our sulks. But retreat into paranoid intimacy can return if we find ourselves in a situation that is profoundly antipathetical to the self. Loyalty to the self produces a sort of *cri de coeur*, an oath made to a loved object, necessitated by embattlement with others who could attack us. As with depressive frames of mind, the paranoid self *feeds* on the negative, a form of intrasubjective breastfeeding; it turns to the breast of dark thoughts and is continuously nourished by them.

This involves a condensation of hateful feelings towards the world outside combined with intense love of the breast that has been constructed to provide succour in the internal world. Listening to the well-named "Rush" Limbaugh is like downing a double espresso of hate. Rush has done the hate work for his listeners, breathing it down his microphone in the voice of "outrage" – a well-named psychological action that is, ironically, a form of unconscious outreach.

In extreme circumstances, an individual caught up in chronic paranoid states of mind may permanently turn inwards and become a recluse, continuously imbibing poisonous thoughts from a dark breast, and celebrating isolation as an end in itself. Tragically, this internal poison can be projected outwards with extreme violence. This could be seen in the school and university massacres that followed from Columbine and Sandy Hook, in which seemingly ordinary kids had bred murderous thoughts towards their friends and then decided to put it all out there, for everyone to see. Mass murder had become a form of confession in America (and then in Norway and elsewhere) that the internal world itself could hatch extreme violence, without a nod to ISIS. Indeed, perhaps blowing the cover of other "perps" around the world, the "lone wolf" American kids who killed friends and revered teachers in model schools in suburban communities, seemed hell-bent on befuddling the American penchant for paranoid reasoning. These were crimes that were not hatched by people who hated America; indeed, they were a part of it. And so, what could be made of this? A quiet challenge was laid out to Americans – and those in other countries – to look inward to find the cause for these seemingly "senseless" murders.

Not everyone enacts their political disenchantment through mass murder. So what else are the millions of infuriated selves supposed to do? Perhaps they can find strength in numbers and a murderous form of politics that channels paranoid rage.

When political movements are based on paranoid ideas, the group process becomes all the more dangerous, as isolated selves discover that there are millions of other people who share the same views. The retreat into paranoia then becomes even more deeply assuring and confirming.

People who opt for a projective solution to the problems caused by complexity, know unconsciously that they have annihilated the group of ideas that do not fit into their paranoid narrowing of reality, together with the people who espouse them. The problem is that some of those ideas and people will previously have been objects of affection or even love. A young man who is converting to radical Islam through paranoid isolation (finding his Rush Limbaugh in ISIS propaganda films) suffers from the breaking of love relations that comes with this mental move. Channelling love towards the new cause, and towards his fellow haters, allows the self to sustain love alongside powerful hate.

This is a striking and powerful throwback to the love and hate felt by the normal infant for his mother. When in physical or emotional pain, an infant will go into a rage and may for a time be inconsolable by even the most loving of parents. A frustrated toddler may blame the father or mother for a psychical situation that is entirely endogenous. But in time this splitting of the loved and the hated, the good mother–father and the bad mother–father, becomes integrated, and the child gradually realizes that the parent who is sometimes hated is the same parent who is also, for the most part, loved.

Melanie Klein called this the "depressive position" – a rather negative term for a positive maturational step – because to have these realizations is to be sobered by the reality of perception, and to be deprived of the joy of full-on hate and full-on love. In the paranoid movements we are discussing, therefore, we can see how the self gains a blissful return to a golden age in which it was normative to hate with fulsome embodied rage, and at the very same time to love with deep, passionate adoration of a sacred object.

Indeed, the arrival at a familiar place where these passions can co-exist, such as at a Trump rally, seems to furnish further mental proof of the validity of the paranoid process. For with love and hate operating in tandem like this, who could ever suffer defeat at the hands of the mealy-mouthed Democrats? Those who aim to oppose it threaten the bedrock of passion itself.

We turn now to another type of paranoid process, one that is harder to perceive. Unlike *positive paranoia*, in which the self espouses a clear view of the world, this is *negative paranoia*, where selves become ostensibly empty of personal views. These are replaced with a mission: to embody a blameless self, opposed to the vulgarities of life and allied with all that is virtuous. In its own way, negative paranoia is also a response to the demands of complexity, and it too constitutes an attack on the democratic imperative.

Positive paranoia is most often to be found in right-wing movements, whereas negative paranoia is more typical of a certain disposition within the left wing. Paranoid right-wing thinkers ascribe evil intentions to those on the left; their left-wing paranoid counterparts occupy a position of sublime innocence, using common phrases to denounce others, implicitly exalting the self.

I attended the University of California, Berkeley during the Free Speech Movement in the 1960s, when many faculty and students played with the imagery of the polis of fifth-century Athens. We were a growing democracy, each person having an equal right to speak on the steps of Sproul Hall, or in any of our other meeting places. Unlike the anti-Vietnam War movement soon to follow, the FSM drew students of all political persuasions and backgrounds; it was limited to a very specific protest – the right to speak freely – and when that goal was accomplished, the movement disbanded.

Returning there in 2016 as a visiting lecturer, I was surprised to hear that the university was then in the midst of a so-called "anti-free speech movement". Faculty were regularly being reported by students for "micro aggressions" and it was having a chilling effect on everybody's ability to think and speak freely in the classroom.

The term "micro aggression" was coined in 1970 by psychiatrist and Harvard professor Chester M. Pierce, to describe unconscious insults and verbal injuries committed against African Americans. It was later adopted, and per-verted, by the emerging "victims' rights groups" that capital-ized, both literally and figuratively, on what they perceived as any slight or aggressive gesture made by one group against another. By the second decade of the twenty-first century this movement was sweeping across university campuses in the United States.

At Berkeley and elsewhere, a micro aggression could be any statement made by a lecturer that might be upsetting to any student in the room. In order to prevent anyone from feeling offended or "traumatized", faculty now had to issue "trigger alerts" before saying something that could potentially be disturbing. For example, before reading from Yeats's poem "Leda and the Swan", an instructor had to inform the students that the poem contained sexual material.

An intriguing strategy used by some extreme members of the anti-free speech movement is the cultivation of what we might term "the dead face": the intentional removal of facial expression. It must have taken a lot of practice to eliminate frowns and smiles, visible recognition of any other, or any spontaneous visible response. This form of radical facial politics demonstrates a refusal to accept the terms of any other's projection of thought or feeling. It is a statement that this person would under no circumstances be subjected to the gaze of the other, as this would be to subjugate the self to the other's ideological system. To be without expression is to rise above this oppression in an act of disconcerting defiance.

Doubtless this position is the result of thought and political reasoning. It is certainly a way for people of all races and cultures to oppose incarceration in the friendly but unconsciously proprietorial gaze of the other, who does not wish to see the self return a smile, but demands it as a condition of social congress.

But context in politics is everything, and whilst the dead face is no doubt an effective and legitimate form of resistance in a context that warrants it, it becomes a problem when selves freelance resistance to become an ornament in itself. This would be the politics of protest, intended to be sufficient in itself or to intimidate all others by use of the self as threat, an alternative to those on the right who bear arms in public in order to intimidate those who are unarmed.

A seminar participant who sits through a lecture with a dead face intends to be intimidating in a different way from the gun-toting self. One side exploits the Second Amendment to bear guns, the other uses the First Amendment to legitimize the freedom to express the act of intimidation. Both sets of actions, however, have chilling effects in their respective environments and cultures and that is the desired effect. Both elicit paranoid anxieties in the group surrounding them: it is their way of exploiting the paranoid element and using it to gain leverage in group relations.

The dead-face movement may be an example of sanctimonious rectitude. Unlike the paranoia of the right, it does not involve the projection of unwanted contents. Instead, it sanctifies its members at the expense of others in an act of extreme self-idealization. The dead-faced people walking around the campus are letting everyone know that they will take nothing from, nor give anything to, the contaminated human environment within which they live. Dead face is prima facie evidence of a self with nothing inside it; a self which therefore, by definition, must be incapable of holding dubious views. Sanctimonious rectitude is the politics of exhibitionism in which being seen to say the right things – always in opposition to a vilified other – is the ticket to the village of saints. It is one of the reasons why the left tend to be much better at public marches than those on the right. Marching has everything to do with the visuality of purity and innocence, and taking to the streets with radiant smiles is very different from marching with furrowed brows as if trooping off to some imminent battle with evil forces.

The negative paranoid position exploits the nationally treasured metaphor of America as "a city upon a hill" that will "cast its light across the ocean" to serve as a beacon of righteousness in an evil world.

The power of self-beatification – using the contrast between one's self and all others in order to leverage saintliness in one's direction – is sustained throughout American history, in spite of plenty of evidence to the contrary. Many historians, notably Richard Hofstadter,[1] have noted the paranoid process that underlies such self-righteousness. The need to be a glorious innocent can reach delusional proportions, at times seriously impairing America's grasp of national and international realities. For however enhancing it might be to feel proud of one's nationality, when it reaches this point it becomes a form of blindness that can imperil both itself and the rest of the world.

Whereas the positive paranoid is *full* of highly contentious opinions, the negative paranoid is rigorously and meticulously *empty* of any views, other than those that serve to negate the other. Most people at times fall into the realm of either positive or negative paranoia, both attempted solutions to the problems posed by existential and social complexity.

Neither mental state permits participation in the democratic process, as neither is able to reflect upon and make use of ideas that are foreign to its own view. However, such frames of mind are part of a dynamic internal world – the self actively seeking to solve a problem – and they will therefore be labile and subject to potential change. It is generally possible for an individual to choose to opt out of such a position.

We have discussed how individuals faced with complexity may unconsciously tend towards paranoia because it simplifies matters. It also bears on that issue which identifies the political right in Europe and America in 2017: the fear and hatred of immigrants. That fear may exist in people in places such as Montana or Iowa, Northumberland or Cornwall, where there are virtually no immigrants. A Congressman from Iowa declared he wanted to live in an America "that is just so homogenous that we look a lot the same".[2]

Although this looks like, and is, a form of racism, it is an ordinary response on the part of anyone to the arrival of a stranger into the community. A group that has met for a year of therapy may react to hearing that a new person is to join them with differing responses – one member might say "that's great", others might provide a more muted response, and some would say nothing. In fact no one wants to take on the unknown.

Unfortunately, paranoid retreat from complexity fates the paranoid to live within an increasingly isolated enclave, even if they are joined by millions of fellow recluses. In retreat from all who do not share the paranoid's vision of reality, he regards others as "aliens" who threaten the hegemony of paranoia. Indeed, *anyone* with other ideas is a migrant seeking to cross the borders of the mind. They must be kept out at all costs because they threaten the paranoid's construction of a defensive identity. This has been effective in providing the paranoid self with a powerful and pleasurable sense of cohesion in a world that otherwise seems contaminated by its opposite: by plurality.

A pluralistic vision drains the paranoid of the security provided by hatred of others. Confronted by *other* views, the paranoid feels – and indeed is – under threat, because the engine of paranoia depends on getting rid of unwanted contents, not on including the undesirable. It is a strategy that finds strength in the pleasure of its power. And once up and running it is exceedingly difficult to alter, unless those in this frame of mind can be brought into consistent verbal contact with selves who hold different views.

We turn now to the calcified trace of psychotic processes: to ideology.

Ideas that have been formed during mad times may remain dormant for decades or centuries, their *raison d'être* long gone. They may be revived by individuals who are not disturbed – not paranoid for example – but their coherence (their simplification of complexity) is attractive to those who wish to expedite matters for the sake of political advantage.

This book has sought to trace the development of certain frames of mind in the Western world over some two centuries. It has examined the paranoid frame of mind – always a possibility during any historical era – that has become increasingly attractive to Americans, who are cut off from the rest of the world in the first place, given to sanctimonious rectitude, and who habitually project their destructiveness into other nations whom they then fear. Although America profited from World War Two, and could claim sainthood for its role in defeating fascism and for the post-war generosity of the Marshall Plan, it had also deployed the atomic bomb, thereby releasing into the world the scourge of the most dangerous weapon ever invented.

In inheriting the wealth of other nations, as well as world domination through its "military–industrial complex", the United States ingested a manic denial of the oppressive politics in the West that had ravaged the world for two centuries and launched Europe and then the rest of the world into its most destructive wars. It was now the "world leader", but what was it leading? It led the way in a downward moral spiral that put profits before people, war before peace and blindness before insight.

Notes

1 See Richard Hofstadter. *The Paranoid Style in Paranoid Politics*. New York, Vintage, 2008. See also David S. Brown. *Richard Hofstadter: An Intellectual Biography*. Chicago, IL, University of Chicago Press, 2006.
2 See Theodore Schleifer. "King doubles down on controversial 'babies' tweet", CNN, 14 March 2017. www.cnn.com/2017/03/13/politics/steve-king-babies-tweet-cnntv/index.html.

14

Ideology

The ideas generated by a political movement that has passionate popular appeal may well outlive its creators, often becoming combined with related axioms from a previous era. As we have seen, the passionate frame of mind that originally drove the ideology may have operated according to a paranoid process, but eventually these disturbed elements may disappear from view, whilst the axioms set in place live on. This means that what began as an emotionally driven position can end up as an accepted set of political points of view. This happened, for example, in Russia, when the Bolsheviks put their lives on the line for what would become the Soviet Union.

Sometimes an old ideological position may be reanimated, decades or centuries later, by the emergence of new passionate advocates, and certain ideologies can function as emotional and psychic holding environments that help to structure people during periods of great turmoil.

Take the idea of "deregulation". This neo-liberal principle proposes that governments should reduce their regulatory function. Although capitalists had never been enamoured of regulation, opposition to it increased markedly in the United States during the McCarthy era, followed in the 1960s by the politics of the John Birch Society and other groups on the far right. These fostered the delusion that the federal government was part of a communist plot to destroy the individual freedoms of Americans. George Welsh, founder of the John Birch Society, even stated that President Eisenhower was a communist agent.

McCarthy sought to regulate the permissible views of American citizens, and the extreme right that followed him aimed to take ideological control of the country. When they unconsciously objectified their ambitions by taking up arms against the government, accusing it of being overly controlling and regulating, we see projective identification feeding a paranoid fear.

This extreme hatred of the federal government can still be found in certain parts of America, especially in the Western states of Montana, Idaho and Nevada, where paramilitary groups, dissident ranchers and other malcontents continue to rationalize their paranoia. They feel suppressed by a powerful, dominating governmental authority, and they have no tolerance for other views.

But the animosity of neo-liberals towards regulation is not necessarily driven by hate. President Reagan's theory of "trickle-down" economics stated that everyone would benefit from those with great wealth at the top of the economic chain, as the money would trickle down to the middle and working classes. This became an ideology that defined the Republican Party, and it had considerable appeal to many Democrats as well.

A political critique of this position might be that deregulation is simply a means for corporatism to flourish and for the wealthy to become richer. A psychoanalytical view might be that this theory is an objective correlative of the psychology of its proponents. In other words, those who think this way have already undergone mental deregulation and are now without proper internal regulatory functions.

The political view that deregulation is efficacious could be considered naïve rather than paranoid. However, a political psychology informed by psychoanalysis could function to objectify malignant transmissions from disturbed states of mind to social axioms, and to persuade individuals and groups to stand back and think about the ramifications of the logical paradigms that underpin political doctrine.

Deregulation as an axiom does not apply only to the removal of a government's regulatory functions; it disseminates more widely into a rejection of all forms of self and social regulation. Trump's shameless expression of racist and sexist views is a manifestation of what happens when an individual abandons self-regulation. If this becomes widespread, it can result in a society governed by id capitalism and primitive states of mind.

Many people have wondered whether those on the extreme right actually believe what they say. Surely it would be wrong to suggest that all the members of the Republican Party are cold-hearted sociopaths when it comes to healthcare provision in the United States. Yet, despite endless statements to the contrary, their position seems to reflect a true lack of concern for the health needs of Americans. How do we understand this?

In fact, the ideologies of reducing taxation and federal regulation at all costs preceded the present generation, but by 2017 they had become axioms that predetermined their approach to many issues. Regulation, they argue, is the enemy of freedom. Government is trying to take something away from us. These were seen, not as opinions but as identifications of reality, so their minds were closed.

The feeling that powerful forces in our world have taken away something that was cherished brings a sense of loss, grief and mourning. And imbricated in the logic of this loss are additional feelings, of abandonment, isolation and helplessness.

Post-war America enjoyed twenty years of unparalleled growth and power. Whilst European and Asian countries were still recovering from the ravages of World War Two, it was as if the United States had been galvanized by that conflict and Americans enjoyed a new prosperity. By the early 1970s, however, the boom waned, and although Americans continued to idealize themselves, the reality was that Europe and Asia were modernizing, producing infrastructures that by the end of the twentieth century left the United States trailing.

Americans felt abandoned. The country was still generally held in high esteem, still seen as the "leader of the free world", yet they only had to look around them to see that other countries were now leaving them behind. Their self-inflated sense of invulnerability had let them down; they were threatened with a sense of depression and this was expressed in a move to blame the federal government, the people they had trusted to lead the nation.

As with all psychodynamic depressions, the experience of abandonment leads on to a loss of belief in the self. However challenging our lives and whatever our situation, belief that we are doing the best we can even under difficult circumstances is crucial to our psychological well-being. If we feel we have failed to live up to our own standards then there is a drop in our self-esteem, and if this is not reversed by existential or psychological recovery or both, this can snowball into an avalanche that leaves us feeling helpless. In an individual, we refer to a total collapse in the self's functioning as a "clinical depression".

There is a collective mourning currently endemic in Western cultures, and further afield, and this involves a loss of belief in cherished values and standards. When societies have been strongly identified with lost beliefs, this can cause a collective loss of sense of self. It seems that the catastrophes of the twentieth century may have left much of the world in the ideological equivalent of a clinical depression.

The profoundly depressed individual might stay in bed, hiding under the covers and ruminating on the self's uselessness. The cultural equivalent might be for people to become preoccupied with the premorbid state of their political, social or religious convictions, perseverating about how fruitless it is to try to influence the course of local, national or world affairs. This may be a depression shared by cultural groups in different countries, the sense of loss objectified in different ways, and sometimes through violence, both physical and emotional. Extremist views may represent extreme forms of dismay.

There have been many forms of politically generated depression. For example, Southern Methodists felt betrayed by the liberal Alliance of Churches, which abandoned many long-held beliefs: that God existed as a Being; that there was a Heaven awaiting the righteous; that heathens and sinners would burn in Hell. They even gave up the idea of Satan. Their revolutionary view that God was more of an idea than a reality and that Heaven and Hell were merely the artefacts of faith left millions of fundamentalist Christians around the world dispossessed. They felt helpless, depressed – and angry.

And around the globe we could find various enclaves of people similarly caught up in a vicious cycle: a sense of abandonment sponsors a feeling of loss and betrayal, followed by a debilitating mourning that renders selves and their communities helpless.

One way out of this dilemma is to transform helplessness and depression into anger. Although anger in isolation is ineffective, if it can be directed at an enemy, and especially if this enemy is shared with other dispossessed people, individuals and communities can emerge from their paralysis and regain a sense of power, dignity and direction.

Born again. *Zing.*

We can learn many things from the negative transformations undertaken by extremists, whether they be radical Islamists, white racist Christians, paramilitary groups who hate "the Feds", or even sedate British citizens who came to hate the immigrants and the EU, and voted for Brexit. (And it is worth noting that for projection to work there has to be some truth to the transfer of blame.) Fear, failure and impotence is a cocktail of emotions endemic to the marginalized. When this matrix is projected, this can become a psychic firestorm that feeds off its own success, a paranoid solution that can be profoundly hard to mitigate.

The unemployed coal miner in West Virginia, unable to pay his bills, living in a lean-to in the woods with his wife and kids, hears in Trump the promise to "make America great again". Through his persona and his prose, he offers a rhetoric that promotes change through rage: we will drain the swamp in Washington, put crooked Hillary in jail, and all will be well. As the despondent miner hears these promises, the disabled parts of the self sense the prospect of cure, and even before Trump has won the candidacy, his vaunted restoration of broken selves feels like proof that he has the solution to America's problems. And the rage directed towards the swamp or crooked Hillary will quickly turn against anyone who suggests otherwise.

This is a *psychological* problem. Although it must also be addressed from many other vantage points (economic, environmental, human rights, etc.), if we do not understand the dynamics of this collective psychological "charge", we risk losing contemporary societies to explosive entropy.

15

The pieces of the puzzle

I began this study by noting the emergence of a manic frame of mind that permeated Europe and then America in the nineteenth century. The revolutionary leaps forward in industry, technology and military power intoxicated nations with a heady grandiosity, and this powerful shift in society overwhelmed matrices of belief held over many centuries. A meaningful life was decreasingly represented by the fulfilling of one's position in the social fabric – as a parent, friend or community member – or in that sense of measure in which selves find meaning in the creative life, whether through a vocation or through work, be it as a craftsperson, teacher or assembly-line worker. Spiritual and humanist pursuits – in the religions, in fulfilling dreams of living an interesting life, in the challenges posed by self-reflection – declined, giving way to the compensatory: in particular, to the search for material accomplishment, the accumulation of wealth and power as an end in itself.

The search for meaning involves a particular relation that each person seeks and establishes with themselves, and for many it may never rise to the level of objective thought. It is rather a sense that one's being is imbued with witnessed purpose, as if we are watched over by a muse who guides us through our life. In the lives of writers or painters that figure may be well known as an imaginary presence but, from a psychoanalytical point of view, we might say that most of us feel guided by the unconscious trace of a caring other, an internal sense and function that we owe originally to our mother. This maternal presence will express itself in our relation to an internal companion, as we transform our mother's love of us into our love of an ideal self that would fulfil her wishes.

Eventually the sense of seeking, and being looked after by, a caretaking other permeates the relationship of our self to our mind. We look to our mind to help us sort out an infinity of problems, guiding our self (consciousness) through the complex matrix of everyday life and its transcendental spin-offs – reveries, inspirations, and the dreams to follow that night. This suggests that the search for meaning has always been connected with the renewing rediscovery, throughout our existence, of a form of love – the loved self – that was there in the beginning of our lives.

For Martin Buber, this muse was God. In *I and Thou*, he wrote: "There is divine meaning in the life of the world, of man, of human persons, of you and me." That relation which yields a sense of divine meaning requires what we might think of as a "local habitation and a name", a certain kind of inner stillness that accompanies the solitude of living. With the ruptures begun with the Industrial Revolution, we have been torn out of many historically meaningful environments, but perhaps the greatest loss has been the relation we have always had to our self as an object of love and care.

We have less time for this now and little transgenerational memory of it.

In the nineteenth century, caught up in the thoughtless greed and industrial power of capitalism, selves were subsumed by the eros of mass psychology, giving themselves over to a collective manic state that propelled them with psychotic exuberance into the Great War. The reality of this war shattered the manic mood, and when Europe emerged from its depressive aftermath, it was never to be remotely the same again. All the beliefs that humankind had developed – from the Judeo-Christian faiths to humanism, from Enlightenment axioms to progressive liberalism – were rocked. The muse unconsciously sought by all of us was displaced by the maddening crowd and the din of militarism.

Writers, philosophers, musicians, artists and sophists reacted with something of an "all hands on deck" approach – they were an avant-garde trying to get ahead of the future

– and for some twenty years, society's depression was met with a sort of counter-mania. But such efforts would not last. The Europeans had learned nothing from the Great War, and after their victory over Germany their psychological ineptness set the stage for World War Two.

This book has discussed how certain seminal writers had previously registered profound psychic changes. Virginia Woolf notes a change in personality in 1910; in 1922 T.S. Eliot describes us as "hollow men" living in a "wasteland"; in 1926 Ernest Hemingway views the Great War as castrating men, rendering them incapable of loving women. In 1942, Albert Camus writes that we are left with one sole question: whether or not to commit suicide. These writers saw a West that had once believed in itself becoming lost: sexually impotent, relationally destroyed, emptied of the human soul.

The aftermaths of the Great War and World War Two produced a waning of self-reflection, self-examination and self-accountability. The values, shaped cumulatively over the preceding centuries, which assumed that human life was inherently meaningful and mentally progressive, were now displaced. We embraced our industries, our capitalisms and the new social structures that gave us prosperity, but increasingly we abandoned our conscience and entered an underworld populated by the most destructive elements of human nature.

The logic of pre-war mania had been to deposit unwanted parts of the self into an enemy, whose annihilation would then create a feeling of righteous cleanliness. In the lead-up to the Great War, Germans certainly felt a sublime aestheticism of self, and this was to reach its apogee in Nazi ideology, which proposed a pure Aryan race, striding heroically across the globe, trampling the faecal remnants of mankind that must be evacuated in order to purify the self. Although Germany lost the war, it can be argued that it advanced the possibility of a structural division between a pure nation and an impure nation. Psychoanalysts might say that this idea was transferred from German self-idealization to the Americans, the Soviets and others, unconsciously and with nuanced differences, but still with a compelling logic.

This manic-depressive division did not manifest as a conscious affective state; it had become structuralized – it was simply part of the order of things. The West split off its depressive side and projected it first into the colonized world and then their own working-class populations, whom they then dominated. The manic aspect was embodied in the military and industrial complexes of the West and the Soviets. For manic forces to retain their position, they must continue to accrue power and domination, and id capitalism afforded those in power nourishment for their greed.

World War Two, the atomic bomb, the Holocaust and the Korean War ended the rosy pictures writers and political leaders could paint about humankind. Although the USA celebrated victory and enjoyed remarkable post-war prosperity – a prosperity eventually disseminated to Europe and the Far East – this luxury was based on what Scheidel[1] terms "mass mobilization warfare": the annihilation of millions of people reduced "wealth inequality" and became "the great leveller", as the gap between rich and poor was reduced through killing.

Over the next half century, billionaires would return to running the world, largely out of sight and often out of mind. The sense of guilt endemic to being part of this manic power structure – the guilt of those who clearly benefit from the current neo-liberal system and libertarianism – was offset in part by conspicuous acts of philanthropy. The Mellons, Rockefellers and Morgans of the twentieth century were followed by the Gates, Buffetts and Zuckerbergs in the twenty-first. A "protective shield" was set up between the dominant class and the ordinary citizens, supported, ironically, by a widespread popular idealization of these giants of industry and capitalism.

In response to the manic-depressive splitting in the mid-twentieth century, a new form of personality emerged. The borderline mind was divided into two parts – one that perceived the world as idealized and another that could register only the negative. It was the perfect reflection of the split in society. The idealizing part of borderlines leaders could love the manic side of their leaders, as we see particularly in the right wing, when the oppressed love and admire their oppressors. The negative part of the borderline, usually found in the left wing, would seek out the depressing dregs of existence, feeding off misfortune and identifying with a powerful grievance and sense of outrage.

The aim of borderline splitting is to allow both states of mind to co-exist in the same personality without ever communicating with one another. When a society divides in accordance with borderline logic, the split generates the extreme views on both sides, making it impossible for the right wing and the left wing to communicate, even though both views actually co-exist in the same "body".

Although the existentialist movement mourned this horrific trend, and tried to find some redemption within its terms, it failed. Sartre offered some consolation, suggesting that our lives still had one precious feature: we were free to decide how to think and how to live. And in his answer to his own question about suicide, Camus suggested another: in our decision not to kill ourselves we find a redemption through a vote against a negative. But these philosophical solutions eventually fell on deaf ears.

If the pragmatic and utilitarian worlds of empirical philosophy, along with their psychological correlates such as behavioural modification theory and cognitive behavioural theory, continued apparently unaffected by this psychosocial turbulence, they did so because they had always eschewed the "larger issues" of life, denying their relevance and even their existence. If there was no self anyway, how could we be in mourning?

The phenomenologists and structuralists, followed by the postmodernists, tried to find meaning in the dense fabrics of their theories, but in the end they were exhausted by this and expired – not with a bang but with a whimper.

The left sought relief in identity politics. At first it was civil rights, then women's rights, then gay rights, and then as the decades rolled by more and more groups of people made valid claims for their group identities in a world often hostile to their causes. Inside these movements too, however, splitting was enacted. We can see in the psychodynamics of identity politics a collective effort to find meaning, but this was achieved through a narrowing of the issues. People would define themselves as a black person, a woman, a gay man, a lesbian, a transgender or as the victim of something – alcohol, anorexia, drugs, gambling. Identity groups might try to form "rainbow coalitions", and in doing so created Kumbaya moments that generated good feelings. But by choosing to affirm a special and separate identity, there was always the risk of losing sight of a wider and more embracing goal: a collective alliance of humanism with science, politics and religion, which might bring together millions of people with otherwise disparate cultures and identities, joining forces to face the challenges of the wider societal psychodynamic.

From the 1950s, in parallel with the rise of the borderline personality came the proliferation of the normopathic self, illustrated vividly in its early twentieth-century incarnation by E.M. Forster in *Howards End*. The normopath takes refuge from loss and mourning by abandoning any wish to explore the inner world, or the wider range of lived experiences to be found under the auspices of "the spiritual". Instead s/he seeks the good life by celebrating material comforts. The joys of driving a car, or going boating, or playing sports, offered an escape from the conundrums posed by the catastrophes of the twentieth century. Whereas the borderline split the loving and the hating parts of the self, the normopath replaced subjectivity with conventionality. Whereas the borderline might suffer profoundly from the effects of his oscillations in personality, the normopath aimed to create an affectless self that would not be tormented.

By dulling intellection and opting for material wealth, recreational pursuits or "new age" therapies, people were aiming to get rid of the mind. The chosen meeting place was no longer the church or temple, the college or university, the local branch of a political party or labour union. In such locations people risked contact with the depressive sides of the societal situation. In order to stay away from the depressions that had now become structuralized, it was as well to steer clear of the bad news industry.

Then came globalization and the advent of IT and AI. The fast pace of social media and globalized interconnections and networking meant that a human response time to fast-breaking news was now redundant. With alarming political and environmental conflicts on the horizon, the fear of our inadequacy left us bewildered, and many sought refuge in identification with the system, as transmissive selves. The psychology of the millennial generation aimed to shield the self from the disturbing mental contents of national and world events by becoming part of the machinery that delivered the content.

Paradoxically, however, the surge of internet users across the globe were now faced with horrifying news brought to them by their own devices. This is the twenty-first-century equivalent to the shock facing the nuclear scientists of the late 1940s and 1950s, who were compelled to emerge from the bliss of identification with the remarkable nature of nuclear fission when they realized the horror of what they had created. The internet, meant to serve our wishes, now turned on us, bringing nightmare scenes of terrorism, political leaders revealed as inept, corrupt, despotic or psychotic, and a world in which climate change was no longer a theory but a deeply disturbing fact.

The factors that have emerged in this study make the rise of Trump hardly surprising. The death-drive backlash against globalization that voted itself into office through his victory, was, in part, a psychological response to a techno-logical world that millions were finding overwhelming. Trump's displacement of scientific and social facts with "alternative facts" spoke for millions of people who found in his garish mania an invitation to mentally annihilate what the world had created. However, as his administration deregulated the offices that governed the country, his act of undoing caused consternation, both nationally and in the rest of the world.

The dynamics of the anti-globalization movement were driven by a paranoid retreat from complexity, allowing selves and nations to feel that militant positions and military might were sufficient to deal with a world that was out of control. Set against this fundamentalist simplification there was a parallel reality in which those who could afford it increasingly split themselves off, living their lives at a distance from the vast majority of their fellow human beings. In these privileged enclaves they were removed, too, from the democratic process. Like Trump, they were creating an alternative reality.

There is no doubt that our world is deeply endangered, both by the threat of nuclear arms and by environmental damage. But perhaps the most serious climate change lies within the human mind itself. Unless we find some way to get selves to come out of their retreats, be it religious fundamentalism or normopathic materialism, our societies will continue to deteriorate and the political process will be emptied of that intellectual vitality and communal effort essential to the survival of *homo sapiens*.

The fight against the pandemic of corruption in all walks of life is not a quaint humanist ambition; it is a crucial form of social psychotherapy in which we struggle to bring ourselves out of a malignant depression that has stripped our societies of their self-esteem, leaving us disabled by the loss of those generative parts of ourselves that had always accompanied us in the quest to create meaningful lives and a better world.

Mentally impaired nations with nuclear weapons and cyber-warfare techniques can make a man-made catastrophe seem almost certain. The quiet evolution of democracy – both as a system of government and as a frame of mind – offers hope. But if we are to exist together, we urgently need to agree new terms for collective life. We may be unable to cast aside our fear and hate of one another, but we must find a way for all players on the world stage to maintain discursive communication.

Democracy is a form of "talking cure", a process that enables people holding very different views to take part in a group mind that embraces and integrates divergent perspectives. Its political priorities are echoed in the various psychological approaches, from psychoanalysis and analytical psychology to Gestalt, transactional analysis, and the theory and practice of group relations. Utilizing the wisdom of these psychologies is vital to the task of understanding the psychological processes that bring nations into war with one another, giving us tools with which to face the irrational bases of our behaviour.

To revitalize democracy, however, we need to confront an unconscious cynicism that pervades the West and other parts of the world.

Trump's victory marked a turning point in Western consciousness. For a hundred years or more, the print media had brought to our attention the corrupt sides of our lives: from the international arms trade to human trafficking and the slave trade; from the corruption endemic to international finance and trade relations to industries – which put profit before human life and health. When Trump boasted that he could shoot someone on the streets of New York and his supporters would still vote for him, he tapped into a dark river of moral bleakness that objectified a shift in Western values.

We had reached a point where we no longer believed in the value of human life and in the ethical mandate that we try to improve the human condition. We had given up on ourselves. In so doing we had abandoned both the individual and the collective search for meaning, and in passively giving in to the emergence of corruption in all areas of life, our manic grandiosity had given way to a collective, endemic depression.

We have changed.

With the loss of a sense of meaning – the feeling that our lives can make a contribution – mourning has turned into melancholia. When we are melancholic we are angry over the losses we have suffered, and we unconsciously blame that which has apparently left us. We now feel abandoned by the humanist predicates of Western culture and the network of belief systems that seemed to offer a progressive vision of humanity, and we have turned our rage against social efficacy itself. This anger takes many forms, from a passive acceptance of all forms of corruption to right-wing identifications with cynical enterprises and murderous solutions.[2]

Those born in the midst of this regression in our civilization are witness to a collective paralysis. Some have cut themselves loose to be "start-ups"; it is a generation left to its own devices as the social fabric that supported prior generations has disappeared. We are now united, not by a

sense of moral purpose but by a shared bleakness – the
"moral crisis" of which the Institute for Policy Studies warns
us. We share the experience of mass bewilderment, dispossessed of a sense of how to find our way out of what seems
the ineluctable end to our species. Millennials may not know
about the sequence of social psychological events over the
last two hundred years that have brought us to this point,
but they inherit the effects. Even though youth will always
try to find the bright side of life, our melancholia seeps into
their veins.

The depth psychologies have always placed a high value
on the examined life, on looking into selves and their societies
in order to gain insight into those mental and social forces
that paralyse us. The democratic process, free of corruption,
offers the only solution, through the use of psychological
understanding and psychosocial change.

A political psychology can help leaders, and all participants in political processes, to rediscover the freedom
provided by the democratic frame of mind. This will require
us to understand why and how we have blamed ourselves
for our losses and given way to masochistic immersions in
hidden forms of self-loathing, but before embarking on that
task we have to reclaim the parts of our minds (individually
and collectively) that we destroyed in the various stages of
our despair. And in order to restore our capacity to think, we
shall first have to confront our widespread psychophobia.

Psychoanalysis and the depth psychologies may be
imperfect but their ambition is not. They are "works in progress" that point towards a crucial function. We have always
known that we needed to "know thyself" and this is as true
now as it has been over the millennia. If we are to reverse
our current state of affairs and preserve our species, it is
essential to realize that, along with the many social causes of
human suffering and disablement, whether economically or
politically determined, our mental life must be taken into
consideration.

If Western leaders can mitigate their grandiose rhetoric
they will reduce the manic substructure that has generated
the malignant aspects of nationhood. By offering a model for
a more modest life, they can create an antidote to greed and

corruption. By declining the mass psychological urge to project a society's destructive ambitions into proxy countries they can substantially reduce the need for militarization and the prospect of war. By expressing regret for crimes committed against other nations they can discover that saying "we are sorry" can provide some healing for the victims of aggression.

This work has attempted to explore a vital need to return to the creation of meaning, in our lives and in our societies, by making use of psychological insight within the experience of democracy. This offers a platform for national and international discourse predicated not on the free market of disturbed states of mind, but on a new form of collective understanding in which humans can turn once again towards becoming humane beings.[3]

Notes

1 See the essay by James C. Scott. "Take your pick", *London Review of Books*, 39(20), 19 October 2017, 23–44. He reviews Walter Scheidel. *The Great Leveler: Violence and the History of Inequality from the Stone Age to the 21st Century*. Princeton, NJ, Princeton University Press, 2017.

2 It would be foolish to underestimate the pleasure we take in greed and violence. The wars and genocides of the twentieth century illustrate all too clearly our penchant for "wargasm": the eroticism of mass murder. This allows us to experience the bliss of total annihilation of human structures and the triumph of the id, as the shadow side of the humane self leads the disturbed sides of personality into victory.

Judith Butler traces CNN's coverage of the invasion of Iraq, which provided, she suggests, an "aesthetic dimension to war" (148). Mesmerized by "shock and awe", the "media becomes entranced by the sublimity of destruction" (149). Any opposition finds it almost impossible to "intervene upon this desensitizing dream machine in which the massive destruction of lives and homes, sources of water, electricity, and heat, are produced as a delirious sign of a resuscitated US military power" (149). See Judith Butler. *Precarious Life: The Powers of Mourning and Violence*. London, Verso, 2004.

Shocking as this "desensitizing dream machine" is, it would be nothing compared to the ultimate wargasm. If Trump were ever to "decide" that he had enough of "Rocket Man" and succumbed to the impulse to wipe him off the face of the earth then "we would all go together": the ultimate in hate-based erotic fusion.

3   The eminent philosopher Martha Nussbaum has proposed and advocated an organization that aims to improve our capacity to bring the better sides of human nature into our group relations. Nussbaum and colleagues advocate what they term "the human development approach", an emerging international movement of people in NGOs and elsewhere who believe in the "capability approach" to improving national and international relations. One of the challenges, she writes is "to work out a political psychology – an account of the emotions and other psychological dispositions that support and impede a program of realizing human capabilities" (180). See Martha Nussbaum. *Creating Capabilities: The Human Development Approach*. Cambridge, MA, Harvard University Press, 2011.

References

Arendt, Hannah. *The Life of the Mind*. New York, Harcourt Brace Jovanovich, 1978.

Atkinson, Anthony B. *Inequality. What Can Be Done?* Cambridge, MA, Harvard University Press, 2015.

Aurelius, Marcus. *Meditations*. tr. Gregory Hays. New York, Modern Library, 2003 [c. 170 CE].

Badiou, Alain. *Theory of the Subject*. London, Continuum, 2009 [1982].

Barbu, Zevedei. *Democracy and Dictatorship: Their Psychology and Patterns of Life*. London, Forgotten Books, 2015.

Bataille, Georges. *Inner Experience*. tr. Leslie Anne Bolt. Albany, NY, State University of New York Press, 1988 [1954].

Bauman, Zygmut. *Liquid Times: Living in an Age of Uncertainty*. Cambridge, Polity Press, 2007.

Bion, Wilfred R. *Experiences in Groups and Other Papers*. London, Tavistock, 1974.

Bishop, Paul. "The unconscious from the storm and stress to Weimar classicism: The dialectics of time and pleasure" in Angus Nicholls and Martin Liebscher (eds), *Thinking the Unconscious: Nineteenth-Century German Thought*. Cambridge, Cambridge University Press, 2012.

Black, Les and John Solomon. *Theories of Race and Racism*. London, Routledge, 2008.

Bleandonu, Gérard. *Wilfred Bion: His Life and Works 1897–1979*. London, Free Association Books, 1994.

Bollas, Christopher. *The Freudian Moment*. London, Karnac, 2007.

———. *The Evocative Object World*. London, Routledge, 2009.

———. *The Infinite Question*. London, Routledge, 2009.

———. *The Shadow of the Object: Psychoanalysis of the Unthought Known*. London, Routledge, 2018 [1987].

Bourguignon, Franç. *The Globalization of Inequality*. Princeton, NJ, Princeton University Press, 2015 [2012].

Boyd, Dannah. *It's Complicated: The Social Life of Networked Teens*. New Haven, CT, Yale University Press, 2014.

Bradbury, Malcolm and James McFarlane (eds). *Modernism*. London, Penguin, 1976.

Bradford, William. *Of Plymouth Plantation 1620–1647*. New York, Modern Library, 1981.

Brown, David S. *Richard Hofstadter: An Intellectual Biography*. Chicago, IL, University of Chicago Press, 2006.

Butler, Judith. *Precarious Life: The Power of Mourning and Violence*. London, Verso, 2004.

Camus, Albert. *The Myth of Sisyphus*. New York, Vintage, 1991 [1942].

———. *The Stranger*. New York, Vintage, 1989 [1942].

Chaitin, Daniel. "Carl Bernstein: Cold civil war media embrace 'different truths'". *Washington Examiner* (online), 16 July 2017. http://washingtonexaminer.com/carl-bernstein-cold-civil-war-gripping-us-as-media-embrace-different-truths/article/2628813.

Coles, Robert. "Psychoanalysis: the American experience" in Michael Roth (ed.), *Freud: Conflict and Culture: Essays on His Life, Work, and Legacy*. New York, Alfred Knopf, 1998.

Conrad, Joseph. *Heart of Darkness* in *Heart of Darkness and Other Tales*. Oxford: Oxford University Press, 2008.

DeLillo, Don. *Cosmopolis*. New York, Scribner, 2003.

Donovan, Lauren. "Tolna Coulee project", *Bismarck Tribune*, 17 May 2011.

Eksteins, Modris. *Rites of Spring: The Great War and the Birth of the Modern Age*. Boston, MA, Houghton Mifflin Company, 1989.

Elliott, Anthony and John Urry. *Mobile Lives*. London, Routledge, 2010.

Eliot, T.S. *Selected Prose of T.S. Eliot*, ed. Frank Kermode. New York, Harcourt Brace Jovanovich, 1975.

Etchegoyen, Horacio R. *The Fundamentals of Psychoanalytic Technique*. London, Karnac, 1991.

Fanon, Frantz. "The fact of blackness" in Les Back and John Solomos (ed.), *Theories of Race and Racism*. London, Routledge, 2008.

———. *Black Skins, White Masks*. New York, Grove, 2008 [1952].

Fonagy, Peter and Mary Target. "Mentalization and the changing aims of child psychoanalysis", *Psychoanalytic Dialogues*, 1998, 8, 87–114.

Fornari, Franco. *The Psychoanalysis of War*. Bloomington, Indiana University Press, 1975 [1966].

Forster, E.M. *Howards End*. San Bernardino, CA, Cassia Press, 2009.

Freud, Anna. *The Ego and the Mechanisms of Defence*. London, Hogarth Press, 1968 [1936].

Freud, Sigmund. "Thoughts for the times on war and death" in *The Standard Edition of the Complete Psychological Works of Sigmund Freud*, vol. XIV, 273–300. London, Hogarth Press, 1955 [1915].

———. "Two encyclopaedia articles" in *The Standard Edition of the Complete Psychological Works of Sigmund Freud*, Vol XVIII. London, Hogarth Press, 1986 [1923].

Freud, Sigmund and Lou-Andreas Salomé. *Letters*, ed. Ernst Pfeiffer. New York, W.W. Norton, 1985.

Fukuyama, Francis. *Political Order and Political Decay: From the Industrial Revolution to the Globalization of Democracy*. New York, Farrar, Straus & Giroux, 2014.

Gasset, Jose Ortega y. *Man and Crisis*. New York, W.W. Norton, 1958.

Grubrich-Simitis, Ilse. *Early Freud and Late Freud: Reading Anew Studies on Hysteria and Moses and Monotheism*. London, Routledge, 1997.

Hadot, Pierre. 1989. *Plotinus or the Simplicity of Vision*, tr. Michael Chase. Chicago, IL, University of Chicago Press, 1993.

Harding, Luke. "It had a big impact on me – story behind Trump's whirlwind missile response", *Guardian* (online), 7 April 2017. www.guardian.com/world/2017/apr/07/how-pictures-of-syrian-dead-babies-made-trump-do-unthinkable.

Hartmann, Heinz. *Ego Psychology and the Problem of Adaptation*. New York, International Universities Press, 1958 [1938].

Hawthorne, Nathaniel. *The Scarlet Letter*. Mineola, NY, Dover, 2009 [1850].

Head, Simon. *Mindless: Why Smarter Machines Are Making Dumber Humans*. New York, Basic Books, 2014.

Hedges, Lawrence. *Listening Perspectives in Psychotherapy*. Northvale, NJ, Jason Aronson, 1983.

Heidegger, Martin. "The Thing" in *Poetry, Language, Thought*. New York, Harper & Row, 1971, pp. 165–82.

Heller, Erich. *The Importance of Nietzsche: Ten Essays*. Chicago, IL, University of Chicago Press, 1988.

Hemingway, Ernest. *The Sun Also Rises*. New York, Scribner, 2016 [1926].

Hofstadter, Richard. *The Paranoid Style in Paranoid Politics*. New York, Vintage, 2008 [1952].

Hollander, Nancy. *Uprooted Minds: Surviving the Politics of Terror in the Americas*. New York, Routledge, 2010.

Ionesco, Eugène. "The Bald Soprano" in *The Bald Soprano & Other Plays*, tr. Donald M. Allen. New York, Grove Press, 1954.

Jameson, Fredric. *Postmodernism: Or the Cultural Logic of Late Capitalism*. Durham, NC, Duke University Press, 1991.

Jung, C.G. "The concept of the collective unconscious" in *The Archetypes and the Collective Unconscious: The Collected Works of C.J. Jung*, Volume 1, Part 1. Princeton, NJ, Princeton University Press, 1977 [1936/37], pp. 42–53.

Kernberg, Otto. *On Borderline Conditions and Pathological Narcissism*. New York, Aronson, 1975.

Khan, Masud. "The concept of cumulative trauma" in *The Privacy of the Self*. London, Hogarth Press, 1974, pp. 42–58.

King, John. "History will ultimately judge. . .I'm a contented man". CNN, 28 April 2013.

Klein, George S. *Perception, Motives, and Personality*. New York, Alfred Knopf, 1970.

Knight, Robert. "Borderline states", *Bulletin of the Menninger Clinic*. 1953, 1, 1–12.

Kohut, Heinz. *The Analysis of the Self*. New York, International Universities Press, 1971.

———. *The Restoration of the Self*. New York, International Universities Press, 1977.

Lasch, Christopher. *The Minimal Self: Psychic Survival in Troubled Times*. New York, W.W. Norton, 1984.

Lawrence, Gordon L. (ed.). *Social Dreaming @ Work*. London, Karnac, 1998.

——— (ed.). *Experiences in Social Dreaming*. London, Karnac, 2003.

Le Bon, Gustave. *The Crowd: A Study of the Popular Mind*. Maestro Reprints (no date or location provided).

Mahler, Margaret. "The magic cap of invisibility" in *The Selected Papers of Margaret Mahler. Volume One: Infantile Psychosis and Early Contributions*. New York, Jason Aronson, 1979 [1942], pp. 3–16.

Masciotra, David. "Pulling the plug on English Departments", *Daily Beast*, 28 July 2014. www.thedailybeast.com/pulling-the-plug-on-english-departments.

Mason, Paul. *Postcapitalism: A Guide to Our Future*. London, Allen Lane, 2015.

McDougall, Joyce. *Plea for a Measure of Abnormality*. New York, International Universities Press, 1980.

———. *Theatres of the Body*. New York, W.W. Norton, 1989.

Mead, George Herbert. *Mind, Self & Society*. Chicago, IL, University of Chicago Press, 1967 [1934].

Melville, Herman. *Moby Dick*. New York, W.W. Norton, 1967 [1851].

———. *Billy Budd, Sailor and Other Stories*. London, Penguin, 1978.

Mill, John Stuart. "On Liberty" in *John Stuart Mill: On Liberty, Utilitarianism, and Other Essays*. Oxford, Oxford University Press, 2015 [1859], pp. 5–112.

Nettleton, Sarah. *The Metapsychology of Christopher Bollas: An Introduction*. London, Routledge, 2016.

Nicholls, Angus and Martin Liebscher (eds). *Thinking the Unconscious: Nineteenth-Century German Thought*. Cambridge, Cambridge University Press, 2012.

Nietzsche, Friedrich. *Thus Spoke Zarathustra*, tr. Adrian del Caro, ed. Adrian del Caro and Robert B. Pippin. Cambridge, Cambridge University Press, 2006 [1883–92].

Nussbaum, Martha. C. *Creating Capabilities: The Human Development Approach*. Cambridge, MA, Harvard University Press, 2011.

Pippin, Robert. *Human, All Too Human*, tr. R.J. Hollingdale. Cambridge, Cambridge University Press, 2005 [1878–1893].

Osterhammel, Jurgen. *The Transformation of the World: A Global History of the Nineteenth Century*. Princeton, NJ, Princeton University Press, 2014.

Phillips, Adam. *Equals*. New York, Basic Books, 2002.

Pontalis, J.-B. *Frontiers in Psychoanalysis: Between the Dream and Psychic Pain*. London, Hogarth Press, 1981 [1977].

Rose, Jacqueline. *The Jacqueline Rose Reader*, ed. Justin Clemens and Ben Naparstek. Durham, NC, Duke University Press, 2011.

Ross, David A. *Critical Companion to W.B. Yeats: A Literary Reference to His Life and Work*. New York, Infobase, 2009.

Salmi, Hannu. *Nineteenth-Century Europe: A Cultural History*. Cambridge, Polity Press, 2008.

Scheidel, Walter. *The Great Leveller: Violence and the History of Inequality from the Stone Age to the 21st Century*. Princeton, NJ, Princeton University Press, 2017.

Schleifer, Theodore. "King doubles down on controversial 'babies' tweet", CNN (online), 14 March 2017. www.conn.com/2017/03/13/politics/steve-king-babies-tweet-cnntv/index.html.

Scott, James C. "Take your pick", *London Review of Books*, 39(20), 19 October 2017, 23–44.

Smith, Barbara Fletchman Smith. *Mental Slavery: Psychoanalytical Studies of Caribbean People*. London, Rebus Press, 2000.

Solms, Mark and Oliver Turnbull. *The Brain and the Inner World*. New York, The Other Press, 2002.

Southern, R.D. *The Making of the Middle Ages*. New Haven, CT, Yale University Press, 1953.

Stampp, Kenneth. *The Peculiar Institution: Slavery in the Ante-Bellum South*. New York, Vintage, 1956.

Steiner, John. *Psychic Retreats*. London, Routledge, 1993.

Strindberg, August. *Miss Julie and Other Plays*. Oxford, Oxford University Press, 2008.

Walters, Joanna. "High gun ownership linked to high rate of police officer deaths, study shows", *Guardian* (online), 14 August 2015.

www.theguardian.com/world/2015/aug/14/high-gun-ownership-killings-police-officers.

Watson, Peter. *The Modern Mind: An Intellectual History of the 20th Century*. New York, Perennial, 2002.

———. *Ideas: A History from Fire to Freud*. London, Phoenix, 2006.

Whitman, Walt. 1855. "Song of Myself" in *Walt Whitman: The Complete Poems*. London, Penguin, 2004.

Winnicott, D.W. *Playing and Reality*. London, Penguin, 1980.

Woolf, Virginia. *A Writer's Diary*. New York, Harcourt Brace Jovanovich, 1982 [1953].

———. "Character in fiction" in *The Essays of Virginia Woolf: Volume Three, 1919–1924*, ed. Andrew McNeillie. San Diego, CA, Harcourt Brace Jovanovich, 1988 [1924], pp. 421–22.

Yaroufakis, Yanis. *Adults in the Room: My Battle with Europe's Deep Establishment*. London, The Bodley Head, 2017.

Yeats, W.B. *The Collected Poems of W. B. Yeats*, revised second edition, ed. Richard J. Finneran. New York, Scribner.

Zaretsky, Robert. *A Life Worth Living: Albert Camus and the Quest for Meaning*. Cambridge, MA, Harvard University Press, 2013.

Žižek, Slavoj. *Living in the End Times*. London, Verso, 2010.

Index

Pages shown in italics refer to information within figures. Information in notes is shown in the format *x*n*x*.